T0375753

# DREAM Model
## to Start a Small Business

EMMANUEL JEAN FRANCOIS

University of Wisconsin Oshkosh

iUniverse, Inc.
Bloomington
Second Edition

DREAM Model to Start a Small Business

iUniverse books may be ordered through booksellers or by contacting:

iUniverse
1663 Liberty Drive
Bloomington, IN 47403
www.iuniverse.com
1-800-Authors (1-800-288-4677)

Because of the dynamic nature of the Internet, any Web addresses or
links contained in this book may have changed since publication and
may no longer be valid. The views expressed in this work are solely those
of the author and do not necessarily reflect the views of the publisher,
and the publisher hereby disclaims any responsibility for them.

Any people depicted in stock imagery provided by Thinkstock are models,
and such images are being used for illustrative purposes only.

Certain stock imagery © Thinkstock.

ISBN: 978-1-4620-2038-6 (sc)
ISBN: 978-1-4620-2039-3 (e)

Printed in the United States of America

iUniverse rev. date: 6/02/2011

# Acknowledgement

I would like to thank from the bottom of my heart my wife Pierrette, and Dr. Margaret Watts (Springfield College) who spent the time to read the entire manuscript and made valuable suggestions to me.

However, any failure in this text is my responsibility.

**Cover image: Designed by Emmarald
and Maellie-Jade Jean-Francois**

To


My beautiful and lovely wife,
Pierrette,

And

My two beautiful daughters,
Emmarald and Maellie-Jade;

And

My handsome boy,
Pierremael.

# Contents

# *Preface to the second edition*

This second edition of *"DREAM model to start a small business"* is published to include minor changes and refinements reflecting the feedback received from the readers of the first edition, especially students, entrepreneurs, and instructors who have found in the book a useful and user friendly companion. Countless of emails received about the book revealed that financial analysis is among the first challenges that new entrepreneurs are struggling with. This second edition includes a chapter completely devoted to financial ratios, which will enable to analyze the profitability, solvency, efficiency, and growth of a small business. I seized the opportunity to add some additional exercises, mostly case studies, at the end of some chapters. I thank you all for your encouraging feedback. I was particularly pleased by those who have used the illustrations provided in this book to start and operate their small businesses. I hope that you will enjoy reading this new edition as well!

Sincerely,

Emmanuel Francois, PhD

# *Introduction*

Someone may start a business without money and succeed. But, even with reasonable capital, an entrepreneur who starts a business without a dream will fail. Being an on-purpose person is a very fundamental criterion to enter the world of business.

Some people started with a dream and failed. They lost sight of their dream. They failed to make the necessary connection between dream and reality. They failed to feed their dream. They failed to visualize their dream. They failed to live their dream. They lost their dream. Dream and reality are two complementary sides of our existence. We cannot afford ignoring either one of them without compromising our chance of success in our everyday endeavors.

The *DREAM model* is a small business start-up approach. Its primary goal is to introduce the reader to the basic concepts related to planning, implementation, and management of a small business. At the end of each chapter, there are some *"DO IT YOURSELF"* exercises to facilitate your learning.

The *DREAM model* outlined in this text is a conceptual framework that provides some simple steps people can use to make their entrepreneurship dream come true. The steps consist of:

- Dreaming,
- Researching,
- Expressing,
- Acting,
- And Managing.

*Dreaming* is the inspirational and intellectual experience that an entrepreneur enjoys when envisioning to start a business. This is the stage where you define your vision and mission statements, goals, and objectives that you want to accomplish. Chapter one is about dreaming.

*Researching* consists of identifying the challenges, aptitudes, resources, and attitudes (CARA) that will enable an entrepreneur to materialize the dream to own a business. The CARA approach suggests a set of questions whose answers will provide critical information to write your business plan and better manage your business. Chapter two elaborates more about this stage.

*Expressing* is an additional step toward action. This third stage of the DREAM model implies the organization of your dream, vision, mission, goals, and objectives into a series of activities through a document called "Business Plan". The expressing stage is illustrated in chapter three.

*Acting* is the fourth stage of the DREAM model. At this stage you develop your implementation calendar, satisfy legal compliance, and process the settlement and operation of business activities. Chapter four underscores the items related to the acting stage.

*Managing* is the fifth and ultimate stage of the model. You don't start a business to let it fail. However, this possibility will be always alive and serve as your companion if you mismanage your business. Although this text is an introduction to the process of starting a business, it stresses, in chapters five through ten, practical information about operations, personnel, financial, information, and risk management.

This text is especially for people who want to start a business. It can be a new business. It can be the purchase of an existing business. It can be a franchise. It can also be an existing business that you want to rejuvenate. The purpose is to help you understand that you do not have to be afraid of your dream. There is a systematic way to put it into reality. Your dream may be too small to accomplish. But, it will never be too big to achieve.

My dream is that this text serve as a jump starter for every business dreamer, every business starter. For almost everything in life, the most important is where you want to go, and the decision to make the first step to get there. Actually, the first step counts more than any other further step. The DREAM model is an invitation to make the first step, no matter what. I hope you will.

Enjoy your reading!

Emmanuel Jean-Francois, Ph.D.

# CHAPTER I
## Dreaming

Obviously the purpose of business is to invest money, time, and energy in one or more activities in order to accumulate the maximum revenue possible at a lesser expense. The positive difference between the revenue (more) and expenses (less) will constitute a profit. Having that in mind, most people are getting involved in the world of business without considering a major factor that contributed for centuries to make most successful businesses what they are. This factor is the dream of the entrepreneur, the dream of the business owner, or the dream of the business manager. Simply put, a business is the translation of a dream into reality. As a dream grows in your mind, it attracts new creative ideas, inspires persistence, urges commitment, and gives the dreamer an obligation to work extra hard to fulfill such a dream.

I have heard people saying so many times that dreams are for the poet, the philosopher or the politician. Some people make that argument not because they can really deny that dreaming is a fact, but because they consider dream as a phenomenon that belongs in a surreal world. Whether you like it or not, your dream will determine the success or the failure of your business. How does dream impact the starting of a business? How can someone concretely use his/her dream to make it useful in starting a business? These are very important questions that the following paragraphs will attempt to address.

## From an idea to a dream

Rebecca and Ed relocated from Boston to Orlando, Florida, seeking opportunities to start a small business. They did not like Boston, because it was too cold there. Before they moved to Florida, they were always whining about wearing a coat every day. They spent a lot for their health care, mainly because of their rheumatism and arthritis. They were looking for a more friendly weather that Florida happens to offer. During the six months after their arrival in Florida, all their health problems seemed to be taken care of by the nice weather. They didn't like the hurricane season. However, when someone asked them how they liked Florida, they answered like a choir, "No complaints! It's super!"

Ed is a very nice man. Rebecca is even nicer. They like making new friends. They like to introduce themselves to new people. They like to visit places that can expose them to new individuals. These are very useful skills or attitudes for people who are interested in business. One Sunday, Rebecca and Ed visited a local church in Orlando. It was not a local church of a couple of members. It was a mega church, which organizes three services with thousands of attendees per Sunday.

After the service, Ed met with some church members and told them that he would like to start a business, but didn't really know what kind of business was appropriate. Curiously, a church member who was listening to him with close attention asked Ed:

"What would you like to do?"

"Honestly, replied Ed, I don't know."

"With all due respect, the man said, I am not sure that you don't know what you would like to do. You do know. Like anyone, you have at least an idea of what you want for yourself. It may not be possible here, but you won't know until you start telling people what you want to do, and what they think about your idea."

Rebecca jumped into the conversation before Ed had a chance to answer.

She said: "Do you think we can open a new restaurant with all the restaurants that I see in the area?"

The man said:

"If you want to start a business, you have to find out what your chances are. I am telling you, a restaurant can be a very profitable business here, if you know what you are doing. I see restaurants come and go. I see some that are very successful as well. One thing I can tell you, people who succeed in business are those who like their business. If you are not committed to what you are doing, you can invest your money, do marketing, and get out of business as a big loser. People in this church are very supportive to new businesses. If they see that you know what you are doing, they will support you as much as they can."

The conversation got interrupted. The people that they were conversing with were about to have an after-church meeting. They left and wished "good luck!" to Ed and Rebecca, inviting them to come back if they had a chance. Ed and Rebecca left the church without accomplishing anything that could eventually help them. They talked about it on their way back home, but were not conclusive. Their conversation switched to another subject, and they never returned to their initial point until they got home.

The reality is Rebecca and Ed left Boston with the intention of opening a restaurant first. However, they were very hesitant, fearing that they could lose their investment if their business is not doing great. Finally they never opened the restaurant. They did not want to take any risk. They put their money in the stock market.

Contrary to Rebecca and Ed, Lacy moved to Tampa from Atlanta, Georgia, with the idea of starting a beauty salon. She is a certified beautician. She has worked in the business for over 10 years. She decided to leave Atlanta to escape the pain of her brutal divorce. Before moving to Tampa, she went to a small business center to acquire information about business opportunities. She hired a consultant who wrote a business plan for her. In addition to the business plan, she collected as many reference letters as possible from people she used to work for. She hired someone to develop a portfolio and a flyer to promote her business. She even printed business cards.

Lacy is a very outgoing person. Like most people who relocate to a new community, she visited the local churches, public libraries, and other public gathering places where she could make new friends. When Lacy meets someone, she gives them her business card, a brochure that features quotes from her reference letters, and tells them about her intention to open a beauty salon.

In about two months, Lacy was able to create a list of 100 potential clients, obtain a fictitious name for her business, a State license, an

Employment Identification Number, and open a bank account. She also rented a well located facility for the business. By the third month of her arrival in Tampa, she had a grand opening for her beauty salon. So far, her business is doing very well with the support of all the new friends that she had already made.

Contrary to Rebecca and Ed, Lacy was able to make it very well. Rebecca and Ed had an idea of what they would like to do, but they did not want to take any risk with their money. They never started a business. Who knows what may happen to their investment in the fragile stock market! Lacy had an idea, and took specific actions to materialize her idea. She was able to start a business that is doing very well. Lacy had something in common with Rebecca and Ed: **an idea**. She had something different from them: **an attitude**, a determination to materialize her idea, by taking risk and being proactive.

An idea can be a simple thought, not well-organized enough to shake the excitement of the common people. An idea can also be a very provocative thought that most people might see as fantasy? or possible only in the surreal world. An idea can be the catalyst for a dream. In other words, a dream may start from an idea, maybe a vague idea, but provocative enough to work in your mind. A non-purposive idea may go out of your mind for ever. But an idea that provides roots for your dream will never leave you alone, until you take care of it. Many successful and famous entrepreneurs who have left incredible business models for the next generations would tell you without hesitation that their dream might have started in an evasive manner. Then, they fought with doubts, fears, and negative perception of others. Then, their dream grew bigger and bigger until they converted others to take the journey with them, and succeeded in the face of all kinds of imaginable social barriers and obstacles.

An idea will become a dream when you obediently let your imagination go on an adventure with it. An idea will become a dream when you block all negative ideas that cross its fulfillment in your mind. It does not cost you anything to let yourself dream freely. The journey that you let your mind travel with your ideas is a very beautiful experience, which can shape your dream into a very exciting vision. Dream and reality are interconnected. A dream is tomorrow reality. The reality is yesterday's dream.

One of the strategies that I usually advise people to utilize as a means to feed their ideas is to voice them out, and record them. It is so simple to stay alone with a tape recorder, and record your ideas. Just speak out! Do not mind about cohesion in your thought! Do not mind about grammatical errors in your sentences! Just let it go! It is time to let yourself be controlled by your true emotion, your dream for your life, your business, your community, or your country, or why not the world.

Keep in mind that some negative thoughts or ideas may try to introduce themselves into your flow of imagination. Speak against them right away, with your firm conviction. If you don't, they can poison your positive thoughts and diminish them while you are delivering. The ideas or thoughts that you let dwell in your mind may finally become your most preferred ideas regardless of their relevance.

Sometimes, it can be very joyful to dialogue with your ideas. The excitement can be felt only by people who actually experience some form of intimacy with their positive and powerful thoughts. When the journey of your imagination stops, you will feel it. You will not be able to imagine with the same ease. This is one of the reasons that I do not encourage people to write down their ideas while they are journeying. The timing can play against you. The time you take to write a sentence can cost you a golden idea. But if you record it, you get it stored. Whenever you decide you can spend some time to listen to your dream, add new ideas that cross your mind while you are listening, or simply transcribing your ideas on paper. This is a creational process. The first ideas that you recorded may be radically modified in the future. However, you have something to build on.

Ideally, you should write down your ideas so you can start to visualize them. You may want to continue in your adventure with further recordings. If you decide to record new ideas, give yourself a deadline when you can start writing them down. You cannot spend all your time in dreaming. Dream is an important part in life. But it is just a part, not the whole life. There must be a time to dream and a time to fulfill the dream.

One of the questions that you may have is "How do I know what my dream is?" You may be afraid to ask this question to other people, thinking that they might take it as a stupid question. This is not a stupid question at all. Any question that someone asks is worth being asked, to the extent that it stresses a need for clarity or more clarity. If you are asking yourself about what your dream is, it is not necessarily because you don't know. It is probably because you are not so certain about it. It can be because you are scared by your current reality. Usually, people try to find logical connections between their reality and their dream. Sometimes, it can be the case. Sometimes it may not be the case. Be careful about how you let your current circumstances influence your dream. They can influence your dream positively by challenging you for a better self or a better situation for yourself. They can influence your dream negatively by creating millions of excuses in your mind and consequently hinder you from moving one step forward.

There are simple things that you can do to identify what your dream is. For example, you can take the time to meditate on the areas of your life, hobbies, and activities that you enjoy the most. Think about if you had full control over these areas, hobbies, and activities! Would you miss a single moment to enjoy them? Of course, not! Why don't you draw a fictitious picture of what you would do for a living if you had all the money and guaranties that you needed? Ask yourself: If I had control over everything, what kind of life would I like to live? Where would I like to go? What would I do with my fortune? What would I like to be recognized for? What kind of legacy would I like to leave? People tend to ask themselves these simple questions. They ask the questions, but they don't take the time to answer them. Don't do that! Write these questions in your personal journal, and write down their answers or whatever answer you can draft. Whatever you would like to become is what you should expect from yourself. I am not aware of any penalty, court, or jail time for people who dream big. You don't have to let people make you believe that your dream is too ambitious. A dream is too ambitious only if you let it sleep and die. A dream alive is never too ambitious.

At first, your dream may appear not clear enough for you. It may sound too much a dream. However, remember that if you can put your mind on it, it is not beyond the realm of possibility. Therefore, don't worry if your dream sounds somewhat foggy. As long as you keep focusing on it, clarity will come with time, dedication, and increase in self-confidence. Obviously, you need to believe in yourself, in your ability to materialize your dream. It starts by translating your dream into a vision.

## From a dream to a vision

A dream can be whatever beautiful picture of a projected reality you want it to be. But, in order to connect your dream with the reality, it must become a vision. Actually, a vision is the limit of your dream. The narrower your dream, the narrower is your vision. The broader your dream, the broader is your vision.

Is your dream to own a "small" local store in a tiny room? You can get it. You will never own a supermarket, unless you change your attitude. Is your dream to own a global competitive corporation? Translate this dream into a vision. If you remain focused on your vision in the proper manner, such vision will be accomplished sometime in the future. Some corporations took decades to become global. Some others just took a few years. You can give any explanation that pleases you to justify why these corporations grew up so quickly. But, you will find other corporations that started at the same time with a narrower vision, but never became big companies. Vision always makes a difference. The ability to visualize what you want to do is very critical for your future success. Visualization can enhance your pragmatism and your sense of commitment. It allows you to dialogue with yourself, and to realize on your own that what you want to do is within reach.

What you need to understand is the fact that a vision will be fulfilled in a timely manner according to several personal and environmental factors that I will explain further. You may start your global corporation in a city. If you remain focused on your vision, sooner or later you will install your subsidiaries in Europe or Asia or Latin America. The fulfillment of a true vision is always a matter of time.

Someone with a vision tends to be resilient. By resilient, I mean the ability to sustain despite adversity. In fact, you always need something strong enough to hang on to when your circumstances seem to worsen. In some instance, the ability to keep your vision alive might be the secret that helps you keep believing in your ability to be successful.

One of the secrets of champions in the sports arena is their vision, their ability to see what ordinary players cannot see. Their vision is different because it becomes a point of focus for them. They do not leave room for distraction. Visualization requires additional mental energy, research, and work. In other words, you cannot be a champion if you don't think and work like a champion. A champion works for extra-hours so she/he can celebrate for a long period of time. This comes with sacrifices, moments of frustration and deception or even short failures. The fact that there is no room for distraction, the encountered frustrations, deceptions or short failures are often metamorphosed into opportunities for growth. An entrepreneur with a vision strives to learn as much as possible about the business, the product, or the market. An entrepreneur with vision pictures the highest quality and uniqueness for a business or a product. This highest standard of quality and uniqueness that the entrepreneur self-develops becomes a point of focus that nothing can influence negatively. It can be painful in the beginning, but may help a business or a product last for ever.

How can an entrepreneur define his/her vision? The answer to this question requires that I ask: What is a vision? A vision is an ideal picture of what an individual, an organization, or a business strives to be at some future time. This is an overall direction, something to be pursued.

Most organizations' visions include:
- A strategic intent,
- A statement of values,
- A statement of quality,
- And one or several indicators of change in a broader community, nation-state or world perspective (optional).

*Example of a vision statement:*

The vision of Clear Copy Services is to be a company leader that provides the best quality and environmental friendly copying services, which enable Florida business to improve their professional image.

The criteria of an effective vision can be identified in the example:
- *A strategic intent*: To be a company leader...
- *A statement of values*: Environmental friendly copying services...
- *A statement of quality*: Best quality...
- *And one or several indicators of change in a broader community, nation-state or world perspective*: Enable Florida businesses to improve their professional image.

## From a vision to a mission

A vision must be narrowed in the form of a mission statement. Unlike a vision, a mission statement is what an individual, business, or organization intends to accomplish. Usually, a mission statement includes:
- A statement of purpose,
- The specification of the clients,
- The business,
- The philosophy,
- And possibly a self-concept.

*Example of a mission statement:*

The mission of Clear Copy Services is to help individuals and businesses improve their performance by providing them quality copying services, in a fast, professional and reliable manner.

- *A statement of purpose*: Help individuals and businesses improve their performance…
- *The specification of the clients*: Individuals and businesses
- *The business*: Copying services
- *The philosophy*: Providing them quality copying services
- *Self-concept*: Fast, professional and reliable manner.

## From a mission to goals

A goal is an end result that a program, a business, an organization, or an institution plans to achieve within a time frame. In other words, a goal must:
- provide at least one outcome to evaluate whether it has been achieved or not,
- set a realistic deadline for its achievement,
- specify the activities, products, or services related to its achievement.

*Example of a goal:*

My goal is to propel the company into a suitable financial position within six years so I can initiate profitable acquisition.

From this example, we can identify:
- *Outcome*: Suitable financial position.
- *Realistic deadline*: Within six years.
- *Activities, products, or services*: Initiate profitable acquisition.

## From goals to objectives

An objective is a specific and measurable activity that must be accomplished in a realistic and timely manner, toward the achievement of a goal. An objective must be SMART, an acronym which stands for:

**S**pecific (A specific activity that can be visualized),
**M**easurable (The activity is measurable),
**A**ttainable (The activity is challenging without discouraging),
**R**ealistic (The activity is achievable within a realistic deadline),
**T**ime-limited (The activity will be accomplish within a deadline).

*Examples of SMART objectives:*

- I will purchase three copy machines within six months.
- I will hire a secretary within eight weeks.
- By May 30, 200x, I will increase my sales calls by 25%.

From example 1, the criteria are met as follows:
*Specific*: Purchase three copy machines.
*Measurable:* Three copy machines.
*Attainable*: Within six months (It will be attainable based on the money available).
*Realistic*: Within six months (If the funding is available, six months is a realistic time to process a purchase).
*Time-limited*: Within six months.

# Dare to be an entrepreneur!

Dare to be an entrepreneur! Mark and Tom had a discussion about what an entrepreneur really is. Mark and Tom have been good friends for over fifteen years. Both of them are retired teachers. They spend their time, sitting on advisory boards of several community-based organizations and neighborhood associations. They never run away from some sort of intellectual discussion anytime they have an opportunity to argue or share their reflection or comments with each other. They engaged in a dialogue on entrepreneurship after a meeting with a group of participants during a workshop for single women who intend to start a small business.

"The meeting was very interesting", Mark said.

"Of course, it was", replied Tom. "However, I think we need to have a serious discussion with them about what an entrepreneur really is."

"Let's face it Tom, one of the basic questions that some of the participants would like us to address is related to a simple definition of an entrepreneur."

"Mark, it is not really difficult to define what an entrepreneur is. An entrepreneur is basically a gambler. Unlike the regular gambler, an entrepreneur gambles smartly. The gambling of an entrepreneur is not based on chance, but on planned risks, self-determination, and the belief that success is the reward of hard working and perseverance."

"Tom, I like your definition of an entrepreneur. It is as simple as it could be. I would probably not use the terms gambler or gambling. However, I get it. I would probably say that an entrepreneur is anyone who decides to initiate and develop a new profit-oriented activity regardless of the risk and uncertainty that may affect such an initiative."

"Mark, you know what, this is great! Both of us agree that an entrepreneur is someone who is willing to take risk in the pursuit of opportunities. I think we can bring this dialogue that we just had into our next workshop. Maybe, some of the participants will implement it with fresh or additional ideas."

As Mark and Tom argued, an entrepreneur is basically a risk taker. This risk taking attitude or ability is based on a dream, a vision, and an ongoing effort to control the outcomes of the risks associated with the business. In other words, you do not take a risk to open a business or send a product on the market just for the sake of taking a risk. A risk worth taking is one that is well researched. A risk well taken is one for which the positive or negative outcomes are predictable to some extent.

## Be an effective entrepreneur!

Our friends, Mark and Tom, whom we met earlier, had another wonderful discussion about what the qualities of an effective entrepreneur are. Using a flip chart, Mark and Tom started to list some qualities related to an effective entrepreneur.

"Tom, an effective entrepreneur is a **risk taker**. When I say a risk taker, I mean someone who can assess the extent of the risk in terms of opportunities and consequences. A risk taker does not invest like a fool, but carefully."

"Mark, I believe that you define an effective entrepreneur as an intelligent risk taker. How about **focus on a vision**? It is good to have a vision when starting a business, but it is a challenge to keep focusing on the vision. The focus on the vision is basically the soul of an effective entrepreneur."

"Tom, an effective entrepreneur is an **optimist**. This is a very critical quality to succeed in business. People may tend to belittle you because of jealousy or lack of appreciation for what you are doing. This can lead to negativism or pessimism if you don't believe in the possibility that tomorrow will be better than today. You may not see the profit right now, but you believe that profit is on its way if you offer quality products or services to your customers."

"Mark, an effective entrepreneur shows **tenacity and courage**. To overcome the challenges of the market, low sales, loss, or accident, an effective entrepreneur will show tenacity and courage to apply what Dale Carnegie said, 'Most of the important things in the world have been accomplished by people who have kept on trying when there seemed to be no hope at all'."

"Tom, an effective entrepreneur has **conceptual ability**. By conceptual ability, I mean the capacity to make in-depth analysis and see challenges in broader perspectives, and suggest solutions that address all aspects of an issue or a problem."

"Mark, an effective entrepreneur is **pragmatic**. This quality helps an entrepreneur take the situations for what they are and deal with them based on documented facts. An effective entrepreneur is very realistic and does not take anything for granted."

"Tom, an effective entrepreneur has a **strong inner drive**, which fuels a passion for quality and success. This inner drive can help an entrepreneur convince others to contribute to an activity."

"Mark, an effective entrepreneur has an **eagerness for learning**. No matter how mindful or clever someone is, there will be ideas that will work, and ideas that are unfit. The eagerness to learn will not only inspire new ideas, but also help avoid repeating past mistakes. An effective entrepreneur has the ability to learn from failures."

"Tom, an effective entrepreneur is **self-confident**. In situations of adversity, an effective entrepreneur shows great self-confidence, which helps cope with difficulties and make wise decisions. An effective entrepreneur has **self-control or emotional stability.**"

"Mark, an effective entrepreneur has **openness for change**. People are naturally resistant to change, because they cannot anticipate what it will bring. However, progress and success cannot happen without change, change in mindset, change in attitude, change in practice. Therefore, it is important that an entrepreneur adapts with change to adjust or preserve the growth of a business."

"Tom, an effective entrepreneur is **competition fearless**. An entrepreneur cannot fear competition. If she/he does, there is no business. Competition helps customer compare the quality of your services and products with these of your competitors, and consequently determines whether you will have a sound clientele."

"Mark, an effective entrepreneur is **energetic and motivated**. Starting or building a business requires energy and stamina, which contribute to the commitment for hard working spirit and attitude. Energy and motivation help not only the entrepreneur, but also people who are working in the business, if any."

"Tom, an effective entrepreneur has **openness to criticism**. Nobody is always right all the time. Therefore, everyone is subject to criticism. An effective entrepreneur welcomes both positive and negative criticisms, and turns them into opportunity for growth. If people criticize the services or the products of a business, an effective entrepreneur does not tend to be defensive, but explore any rationale behind the criticisms in order to make appropriate adjustments."

"Mark, an effective entrepreneur understands the value of **time management**. People who succeed are those who understand the value of time. Thomas Edison said, 'The thing I lose patience with the most is the clock. Its hands move too fast. Time is really the only capital that any human being has, and the one thing that he can't afford to lose.' An effective entrepreneur never misses the opportunity to do something productive with his/her time. Planning is one of the best tools that is used by entrepreneurs to avoid wasting too much of their time."

"Tom, an effective entrepreneur knows how to cultivate **interpersonal relationships**. Of course there is marketing, which can help a business increase sales. However, there is no better efficient tool for an entrepreneur than interpersonal relationships. You will not succeed in business if you cannot establish and cultivate good relationships with your partners, your employees, and your clients."

"Mark, an effective entrepreneur has a **sense of urgency**. The energy and motivation level give the effective entrepreneur a sense of urgency to put ideas into actions. An effective entrepreneur will not postpone any decision that can be made immediately. An effective entrepreneur will not let a critical situation worsen before seeking correction or improvement."

## Beware of the challenges!

It is important for new entrepreneurs to understand that starting a business carries some serious challenges that they should be aware of. The Small Business Administration has made it clear that businesses come and go because they were unable to overcome some common challenges. Our friends Jessica and Sasha had a wonderful dialogue about that.

As Jessica entered the room, Sasha handed her a bottle of water that she purchased from the vending machine. "Thank you!" Jessica said. Jessica tapped on the bottle of water with her pen. Sasha understood automatically that she wanted to say something.

"Hey Jessica, what do you have in your mind, Sasha asked?"

"Why do you think people start a business and are not able to make it through?" Do you think that money is the only challenge?"

"Well, said Sasha, I don't think that money is the only challenge, although it is a big challenge, if not the biggest."

"Why do you think it is the biggest challenge, asked Jessica?"

"Jessica, I would not say explicitly that money is the biggest challenge when starting a business, but it is the most influential factor of business failure. Let me explain what I mean by that. You need capital to start a business. If you don't have it, you are not in business."

"Sasha, I have to respectfully disagree with you. Your statement inspires me to say something different than what you said. I understand that you need money to start a business. You may have money and not be able to start a business if you don't know what you want to do. I mean, if you don't have a vision. However, if you have a vision, and you are committed to that vision, you may be able to generate ideas that will bring you money to start your business. I would say that the lack of purpose, the lack of commitment or insufficient commitment might be the greatest challenge to start a business."

"Jessica, you are right. Nevertheless, I want you to keep in mind when I said money, I meant that money is related to most of the challenges that someone may encounter when starting a small business. I will give you a couple of examples. If you have a vision you can generate ideas to bring money. In some instances, you still need some money before ideas can bring you money. You may have vision and money, but lack of experience can lead to wrong decisions and business failure."

"Sasha, I understand what you said. I think the problem is because we were talking about the greatest or the biggest challenge. I think we should avoid using these terms to the extent that both so-called big and small challenges can make a business fail. We should probably talk about the challenges related to small business failure."

"Jessica, you got it right! I think there is a variety of factors that an entrepreneur should be aware of when starting a small business. The list may include, for example, lack of experience, insufficient capital, poor location, poor inventory management, over-investment in fixed assets, personal use of business funds, and poor credit arrangements."

"Sasha, there are some other challenges that are as much critical. I would say:

- Inability to respond to competition,
- Disappointments in terms of expected progress and profits before starting the business,

- Poor or insufficient planning about the market or a product,
- Narrow mindedness about change and innovation,
- Poor customer service, which can affect the sale of a service or a product,
- Poor time management,
- Poor record keeping,
- Poor quality assurance, which can discourage clients to purchase a service or product,
- Poor risk management, which can lead a business to bankruptcy,
- Overexpansion of the business based on short-term success."

"Hey Jessica," Sasha said," I have to go. I will talk to you later."

"I enjoyed the conversation, said Jessica. We have to do it again!"

## You are ready to go out!

Like Jessica and Sasha, an entrepreneur must understand that there are challenges ahead when starting a business. Challenges are challenges. They can be overcome if you make yourself aware of them, and develop personal strategies to handle them to the best of your abilities.

If you can hold a working paper on which you have written your dream, your vision, your mission statement, your goals, and your objectives, and are willing to develop the attitudes of an effective entrepreneur regardless of the challenges ahead, you are ready to go. The dreaming phase is not passive. It must be a very active process for you. Remember that you have to record your dream, transcribe it on paper, and write a vision statement, a mission statement, and some goals and objectives. Once you have done that, your business is already established. You can go out to research your dream to start your business. Now you have a clear idea of what you are going to research. Of course, the following chapter is about what you have to research as your next step in the process of starting your business.

| **DO IT YOURSELF!** |
|---|
| 1. Write a summary of your entrepreneurship dream in up to 100 words! |
| 2. Write a vision statement that summarizes your dream in up to 25 words. |

3. Write a mission statement related to your vision statement in up to 30 words!

4. Write one goal you intend to pursue to achieve your mission!

5. Write 3 SMART objectives that can help you accomplish your goal!

6. The Smith Shad Case

Smith Shad is a dishwasher working at a fast food restaurant in Naples, Florida. After all deductions, Smith receives $ 1,200.00 per month as his net income. He has another part-time job during the week-end that pays him $ 150.00 per week. Smith has $2,000 on his checking account and $5,000 on his saving account. Every month, he pays $500 per month for rent, $ 80.00 for electricity, $40.00 for utilities, $50.00 for telephone, and $ 80.00 for gas. In addition, he spends about $ 200.00 per month for groceries and other shopping activities.

Smith is dreaming of starting a small business that provides computer and copying services. He is dreaming of hiring a computer technician, a graphic designer, a Microsoft user specialist, and a bookkeeper. He sees his business growing throughout Naples and the State of Florida within 5 years.

Smith said to one of his friends, "My goal is to start a small business with a start-up capital of $ 10,000 within three years". He added, "In order to do that, I plan to (a) Make a 10% take-home pay cut from my net income to increase my savings, (b) Reduce my monthly gas expenses by 10%, (c) Secure a line of credit of at least $ 3,000.00 with my credit union."

Questions

1. Do you think Smith's goals are realistic and his objectives SMART? Explain!

2. Given Smith's income and expenses, do you think he will be able to start a small business within five years? Why?

3. How would you re-write Smith entrepreneurship dream?

4. If Smith were to start his new small business, how would you write the vision statement, mission statements?

5. What are five other objectives that you think Smith could write in relation to his goal to start a small business within 5 years?

# CHAPTER II
## Researching

We have seen in the preceding chapter that dreaming is an important factor in starting a business. In fact, you will never have to lose sight of your entrepreneurship dream. There will be some time of discouragement or loneliness where your dream will be the only real resource available to you. This is probably one of the reasons that you have to match your dream with research. You may probably ask what research has to do with starting a business. This is a legitimate question that you will need to be able to answer for yourself.

## The role of research before starting a business

What is research? Research is a process of providing a solution or attempting to arrive at a solution to a problem through a systematic approach. Actually, a problem can be an issue, a concern or a need. For example, the dream to start a business is a need that has to be researched so that most of the decisions are made in the best possible way.

In fact research can help you find the best type of business that matches your dream. Research can help you identify the resources that are available for your type of business and how to use them. Research can help you identify the obstacles related to a particular type of business. Research can help you find the appropriate location for your business. Research can help you find potential customers and partners to sustain your business. Research can help you find and obtain the funding needed to start or expand your business. You will add to the list while you are researching to start your business.

# Legal forms of business

There are several legal forms of business. The most common are sole proprietorship, partnership, corporation, limited-liability company, trust, cooperative, and the joint venture.

*Sole proprietorship*

A sole proprietorship is a business owned by only one person. The owner of such a business is called a sole proprietor. Most States require that a sole proprietorship transact business under an assumed, trade, or fictitious name. A sole proprietorship needs to obtain an Employer Identification Number (EIN) and comply with applicable sales tax permits and licensing requirements.

*Advantages:*
There are many advantages in opening a sole proprietorship. For example,
- The sole proprietor has full management authority over the business;
- The owner does not have to share the profits;
- The sole proprietor is not concerned by double taxation as opposed to a corporate owner who is taxed twice;
- There are fewer expenses for the organization of the business;
- There are fewer regulations and reporting requirements.

*Disadvantages:*
There are some disadvantages when doing business as a sole proprietor. For example,
- The sole proprietor is solely liable for all debts and obligations of the business;
- It can be very difficult to sell or transfer the proprietary interest of a sole proprietorship;

- The sole proprietor may lack the diversity viewpoints in making management decisions;
- It can be more difficult to raise capital for the business;
- Sole proprietors who run very profitable businesses may pay a higher tax rate;
- There may be no business continuity if the owner dies or ceases to do business.

*Partnership*

The Uniform Partnership Act__ approved in 1914 by the National Conference of Commissioners on Uniform State Laws __ defines a partnership as "an association of two or more persons to carry on as co-owners of a business for profit." The rights and responsibilities of the partners are set in the partnership agreement or the Articles of co-partnership. A partnership is required to file Form 1065 with the Internal Revenue Services (IRS).

There are general partnership and limited partnership. In a general partnership, all partners are liable to the debts and obligations of the business. In other words, each partner is responsible for the acts of the other partners.

In a limited partnership, there are general and limited partners. The general partners are liable to the debts and obligations of the business. The limited partners are liable to the amount of money they have invested in the business.

*Advantages:*
- Unless a partner waives his/her rights, all the partners have equal authority and power to manage the business;
- Less regulatory and reporting requirements;
- Less expenses to organize the business;
- Partners pay single tax (They are not double taxed);
- There is more possibility to raise capital than with a sole proprietorship because of the cumulative value of the personal wealth of the partners.

*Disadvantages:*

- Except in limited partnership, partners are liable to all debts and obligations of the partnership, regardless of their personal involvement;
- Possible constant disagreements among partners can lead to mismanagement problems;
- Possible difficulty to transfer proprietary interest;
- Legal fees to draft good partnership agreements can be considerable;
- Some partners may pay higher tax rate than others;
- Possible problems for the continuity of the partnership, in the case of a partnership at will (The partnership can be dissolved by decision or withdraw as of one partner).

*Corporations*

According to an early decision of the U.S Supreme court, "a corporation is an artificial being, invisible, intangible, and existing only in contemplation of law." In other words, a corporation is an artificial entity created by law. This entity is separate from its owners or managers, called stockholders or shareholders. The corporation itself is liable for any debts and obligations. Requirements to form a corporation vary from one State to another. However, the minimum number of stockholders ranges from three to five.

To form a corporation, you need to:
- Choose a name,
- Define the purpose of the corporation,
- Have a physical mailing address,
- Specify the duration of the corporation,
- Specify the number of shares to be issued,
- Determine the constituents of the board of directors,
- Organize the first meeting to elect directors and officers,
- File the articles of incorporation with your state agency,
- Adopt bylaws
- Obtain Employer Identification Number (EIN),
- Obtain corporate seal,

- And comply with local (County, city) agencies regarding other business requirements and restrictions.

There are several types of incorporations such as:
- *The C corporation*, which is the traditional form of corporation that provides limited liability for the stockholders and double taxation;
- *The S corporation* formed with 35 or fewer stockholders, which exonerates double taxation (non-resident aliens may not be shareholders);
- And *the non-profit corporation*, in which "no part of the income is distributable to its members, directors, or officers".

*Advantages:*
- Except in the case of an S corporation (there may be an exception), a corporation may choose the tax year that best fits its business cycle;
- The stockholders have limited liability;
- The business may continue beyond the life of the stockholders;
- There is more possibility to raise capital;
- The ownership is easily transferable;
- The business is more likely to be managed by the more skilled people.

*Disadvantages:*
- Except for the S corporation, there is double taxation for the stockholders;
- There may be additional taxes depending on where the corporation transacts business;
- There are more legal formalities and reporting requirements.

*Limited-Liability Company*

A limited liability company (LLC) is a non-corporate entity that offers the benefits of both a corporation and a partnership. The owners of a LLC have no liability for the debts and obligations of the business. Owners of the LLC can manage their business unless it is stated otherwise in the company articles of organization. An LLC may be dissolved by the decision of any one member.

*Advantages:*
- There is limited liability for the owners;
- There is no double taxation;
- There is more possibility to raise capital;

*Disadvantages:*
- The business can be dissolved at any time;
- Some States may treat an LLC as a corporation for taxation purpose;
- The ownership is not easily transferable;
- There is not enough uniformity among State Laws concerning LLC.

## Other forms of business

There are other legal forms of business, such as:
- *Joint venture:* Temporary partnership whereby two or more non - competing companies undertake a single endeavor to make a profit.
- *Trust:* A business established for a specific period of time to receive specific assets, hold these assets, and distribute them to the beneficiaries according to pre-determined conditions.
- *Cooperative:* A business formed by independent producers, wholesalers, and retailers to buy and sell collectively for its clients.

## Do your research through the "CARA approach".

Most researchers use research questions that help them guide their research process. I would suggest you to do that through what I call the "CARA approach". The CARA approach is a set of four questions that can guide your research process. The concept CARA is an acronym where:

C stands for Challenges
A stands for Aptitudes
R stands for Resources
A stands for Attitudes

Then, the questions are:
- What are the challenges that face the business that I am dreaming of starting?
- What are the aptitudes that I have as assets to run such business?
- What are the available resources to start and expand this business?
- What are the attitudes that I will have to develop in order to face the identified challenges and take the most advantage possible of the available resources?

## Figure 1
## The CARA approach

| (C) Challenges: | (A) Aptitudes |
|---|---|
| . Obstacles/Barriers | . Strengths |
| . Market profile/needs | . Market knowledge |
| . Economic threats | . Passion |
| . Competitiveness | . Talents |
| . Budget | . Education |
| . Product/service | . Experience |
| . Financial projections | . Past achievements |
| . location | . Leadership skills |
| . Bookkeeping/Taxes | . Management skills |
| . Risks | . Public relations skills |
| **(R) Resources:** | **(A) Attitudes:** |
| . Financial assets | . Customer service |
| . Legal requirements | . Sales/Marketing |
| . Insurance | . Advertising |
| . Funding | . Public relations |
| . Equipment | . Networking/outreach |
| . Stakeholders | . Ethics |
| . Market potentiality | . Employee relations |
| . Professional assistance | . Start up sheet |
| . Providers/suppliers | . Operations |
| . Guides/manuals | . Evaluation |
| . Associations/organizations | . Leadership |

## Discover the challenges

Discovering the challenges implies that you identify all possible barriers, obstacles, threats or risks related to the business that you are starting. There are some more specific questions (not in order of importance) that can help you address your challenges:

*- What is the product or the service that will sell your business?*

An entrepreneur starts a small business to sell a service or a product. The service or product that you intend to sell must be clearly defined in your mind and on paper. You may want to start a new business, enter an existing business, buy an existing business, or purchase a franchise. You should be able to provide a convincing picture of your business when you are discussing with potential partners, clients or lenders. This is what is called your "business concept". If you cannot do that, chances are that people will rightfully think that you don't know what you want to do. It is not a good place for an entrepreneur to be.

*- What is the name of the business?*

Selecting a business name is a critical aspect. My advice is to give your business a name that clearly indicates what kind of services or products that you sell. It is better to keep the name short or have an acronym that is easy to say and remember. Also, you should link the name of the business with a logo that can catch the attention of people. You may want to name your business after you. There is no big deal with that. Many businesses bear the name of their owners. However, remember that your name will not necessarily provide a non-equivocal indication of your services or products. There is another factor that you should consider when the business has the name of the owner. If you sell your business, for example, you risk finding yourself in embarrassing situations should the business get involved in ethical or legal problems while bearing your name.

*- What are the potential customers that need these products or services?*

If you are about to start a business, you should do your best to identify as accurately as possible the profile and the size of customers who will request your services or purchase your products. At least, you should have a convincing response for this question.

*- What are the specific needs of the potential customers?*

In addition to identifying your potential customers, you should know what their specific needs are. If you know what the specific needs are, it becomes easier to assess whether they are met or not. This will help you understand what you can do to underscore and address these needs through the services or products that you will offer.

*- What are the demographic profile, income status, and cultural background of the potential customers?*

The demographic profile of potential customers is very important to avoid offering services or products for a sub-category that don't need them. For pricing purpose, you need to have a good idea of what the levels of income are. This information will be very useful when making marketing and customer service accommodations. You need to know their cultural backgrounds so your services and products are culturally sensitive.

*- What are the actual and eventual competitors?*

It is obvious that every business has at least one competitor. You must know the competitors, locate them, visit their facility, and have information about their products, services, prices, reputation and any additional information that is accessible. Such information will help you define what the strengths and weaknesses of your competitors are. Depending on the market, you should be able to make a judgment about potentiality of eventual competitors and how you anticipate positioning yourself in such eventuality.

*- What are your competitive advantages? How will you take advantage of them?*

When you have information about your competitors, you should be able to determine what your competitive advantages are, and to what extent you can exploit them. Customers or clients should find something in your business that your competitor (s) don't provide. Uniqueness is key for the success and competitiveness of a new business.

*- What are your competitive weaknesses? How will you overcome them?*

When comparing and contrasting yourself (your business) with your competitors, you must stress what your weaknesses are. It does not stop there. You must think and write down strategies that can help you address or compensate the weaknesses.

*- What are the changes in the national economy that may affect your business (Interest rate? Inflation? Etc). How will you respond?*

The fact that you start a business in a small community does not mean that the national trends and changes in economy do not affect that business. Your job now is to determine what the trends and changes are. How will you recognize them? What do you anticipate to do should an unforeseen event occur?

*- What are the political-legal changes that may affect your business? How will you respond?*

Like the trends and changes in the economy, the political-legal environment can strongly affect your business. You need to identify what possible political or legal changes can have an impact on your business. How do you anticipate to responding to these possible changes?

*- What is the appropriate location for your business (Crime rate? Accident rate? Accessibility? Security?)*

You may have the best business ideas, good marketing, and sufficient capital, but fail to make your business prosper if the location is not appropriate. You have to define on your own terms what the appropriate location for your business is. A lot of factors such as crime rate, accident rate, accessibility, and security might be worth taking into consideration. You will find such information on the websites of the local chamber of commerce, the U.S. census, the police department, or the local department of law enforcement.

*- What are the taxes that your business will have to pay?*

Before you start your business, you need to be aware of all your tax obligations at city, county, state, and federal levels. Taxes vary with the type of business that you are starting. Visit the business offices of the city and county where you will do business to find information about taxes related to your business. The website of your state will provide you information about State taxes for your type of business. Information about federal taxes is available at the Internal Revenue Service (IRS) website (www.irs.gov/businesses).

*- What are the licenses that your business and/or the employees (if any) need to have?*

There are basic business' licenses required at the city, county, or state levels in order to start a new business. In some cases, there may be required professional licenses that either the owner or the employees must have before they can provide a service or sell a product. Be aware of what the licensing requirements are through city, county, and state agencies. As indicated earlier, you can either call or visit their office or their website.

*- What is your budget of expenses like?*

You must anticipate what your budget of expenses will be. Usually, you have to do some preliminary research, talk to people who are knowledgeable about the business, and make a list of mandatory expenses. By mandatory expenses, I mean all expense that you have to make in order to operate your business. It can be anything from incorporating your business, purchasing materials and equipment to leasing or renting a location, and similar items. This will help you determine where you stand in terms of whether you can start your business or not.

*- What is your cash flow projection like?*

To the best of your judgment and available information related to the umbrella industry of your business, you must write down a cash flow projection. A cash flow projection is simply the cash that you anticipate will flow in and out of your business. As a reminder, a cash flow projection is not your profit, but the flow of cash related to purchase and sale.

*- When will you have positive cash flow?*

Business cash flow can be positive or negative. Obviously, if more cash goes out than gets in, the cash flow will be negative, and vice versa. You must anticipate in your projection how long it will take you before your business can start generating positive cash flow.

*- What is the breakeven point of your business?*

Positive cash flow does not mean that you have an overall profit from your business. It is an encouraging indicator of how your business is doing. A better indicator is the break-even point. The break-even point is the point when your income equals your expenses. Moving beyond the break-even point means that you make profit. It is important that you know what your break-even points are.

## Discover your aptitudes

I started to say that you have to dream your business before you do anything else. This is because you and your dream are the greatest asset ever for your business. One concrete way this will help you is to identify your aptitudes. Your aptitudes are an investment in your business if you fully take advantage of them. There is no greater source of motivation and determination than self. No external motivation can supersede a strong internal motivation that combines with one's aptitudes. You can discover your aptitudes that constitute an asset for your business by asking yourself and answer the following questions:

*- What have you been most successful at doing? What made them successful?*

Nobody should be able to answer these questions better than you. However, this statement is not always true. Sometimes, people underestimate themselves so much that they cannot make an effective assessment of what their potential is. If you are in that category, you don't have to worry too much. You can do something about it. You can take the time to reflect on your past accomplishments. Ask yourself what personal accomplishments do I feel strongly proud of? What made them possible? Another thing that you can do is to find someone who can be honest with you, without flattering, and ask that person to tell you about what she/he can consider as your most successful accomplishments. You may find another way to answer these questions. The most important endeavor is to have answers for them.

*- What do you like to do the most?*

If you know what you like to do the most, you are not too far from identifying what your entrepreneurship passion could be. When you do something that you like to do, you tend to do it very well. And more importantly, it tends not to be a burden. There is a strong potentiality for customer service there. People like to be served by someone who is somewhat passionate about what he/she is doing. If they see a genuine passion in you, trust me they will naturally come again!

*- What is your level of knowledge of the products or services that you will sell?*

Do you want to provide a service or sell a product? What is your level of expertise about this service or product? You must know. Period! You must know something about the type of business that you want to start if you really want to own one. You don't have to be an expert. However, you may have some basic knowledge about your potential business so you can effectively process information that you are receiving.

*- What is your personal experience with the potential customers of your business?*

Do you have any personal experience with potential clients of your business? You need to ask yourself that question. If you do not have any, this is not a problem. If you do, this is an asset for your future dealing with clients. Any personal experience with potential client can also be considered as a tool.

*- What specific skill(s) in your educational background that can help you in your business?*

Sometimes, people have specific skills that they don't value, but can be of great importance when operating a personal business. Is there any training, workshop or seminar that I attended and is related to my business? Is there any book that I read which can provide me insight or more confidence in operating my business? You may not be able to answer this question. There is nothing wrong with that. However, you will not know if you can answer the question or not until you start reflecting on it. If you do have encouraging answers about this question, ask yourself, "how can I use them in the context of my business?"

*- What activity (ies) in your past experience that is (are) related to the business that you are starting?*

Ask yourself, "is there any activity that I used to do in the past, which is related to the business that I am about to start?" The activities may not be closely related to your business, but may have required skills that can serve as prerequisite for the services or products that you intend to offer in your business. You may not be able to use these skills directly in your business, but they may provide you appropriate reflex to better negotiate a contract, a partnership or hire your employees.

*- What are your leadership skills?*

Simply put, leadership is the ability to influence the motivation of an individual or an organized group of individuals in order to achieve certain goals or objectives. Have you ever been the head of a group of people either as a supervisor, instructor, advisor, or a leader? If you have, chances are that you have some leadership skills. Now is the time to ask yourself "how was I able to influence people?", "What did I do right that contributed to motivate them?", "How can I use these techniques or strategies to better manage my business?"

*- What are your management skills?*

Did you ever manage any previous activity or business? Do you have any previous experience in making plans for a project? Do you have any previous experience in tracking expenses and writing financial reports for a personal or a group activity? Do you have any previous experience in recruiting volunteers or crews for an activity or a project? If you do, you may have some management skills. What are these skills? Take the time to think about them, and write them down. Then, underline the management experience that you think you will need the most to effectively operate your business?

*- What are your public relations/marketing skills?*

Do you have any public relations skills? If you do, you will certainly know. For example, if you used to work with associations in your neighborhood, in a local church or a community based organization, you may have some experience of doing outreach for events. You may transform your experience into public relations or marketing skills.

## Identify the available resources

Running a business is after all a matter of managing resources to make a profit. Then, the research must involve the identification of resources that are available not only to open the business, but also and especially to manage and eventually expand it. You can ask and answer the following questions to identify the available resources for your business:

*- What are your financial assets?*

Once it is clear in your mind that you want to start a small business, you must determine what your financial assets are. By asking yourself this question you will know whether you have enough financial resource or not to start the business. If you don't have enough financial resource, this will suggest to you new questions related to where you are going to find the additional money that you need.

*- What other people's assets you bring into your business? How? When?*

If you have enough financial resource to start your business, you need to identify other funds that may be available if you are in trouble. If you don't have enough financial resource, you have to think about other people's assets that you can bring to compensate your lack. It may be from your spouse, a relative, or a friend. This is an area where you have to be specific, in terms of (a) "Who can I contact?", (b) "How will I frame my request to convince that person?", (c) "When will I need to do that? You may also think about applying for credit cards or a line of credit?"

*- What are the legal forms of business that you can open? Which form are you choosing? Why?*

A small business can be a sole proprietorship, a partnership, a limited liability company, or a corporation. In another context, it can be the purchase of an existing business, or a franchise. What legal form of business do you think is more appropriate for your present circumstances? Why do you think this is the most appropriate form?

*- What kinds of insurance match your form of business? Which kind are you choosing? Why?*

In terms of risk management, you need to explore the kind of insurance available for your type of business. What will the assurance cover? What will be the cost? What are the best providers? These are very important questions that some people neglect to ask themselves until there is a lawsuit, an accident, a fire, a hurricane, or an act of vandalism?

*- What is the available funding for your type of business? Do you meet the requirements to take advantage of them? If not, what is your timely-plan to meet them?*

The Small Business Administration, State, County, and City agencies, the credit unions, and the banks may have funds available in the form of loans. Sometimes, some non-profit organizations have grants available for small business start-up. You need to make for yourself a list of fundings for which your business is eligible. Find out what the requirements are. Then, assess whether you meet these requirements. If not, at what point do you think your business will be competitive to meet these requirements? What will you need to do to meet these requirements over time?

*- What are the available purchase and leasing options for your business?*

In addition to loans and grants, there are purchase and leasing options available for small business that you can take advantage of. You may inquire from different stores and companies; assess what the advantages and disadvantages are. For example, you may not have enough money to buy a copier machine or a printer, and consider leasing one. Of course, you have to weigh whether this is the appropriate decision to make.

*- What are the providers that you can partner with to do business? How will you select your providers?*

When you assess your market and your competitors, you may find that there are other companies that you can partner with to do business. Take some time to research possible providers, their requirements, and determine whether there are opportunities for future partnerships.

*- What is the profile of the employees (if any) that you would like to hire? How will you attract and retain them?*

If you intend to hire employees, they will be your greatest asset. You need to ensure that you hire the best employees possible. Ask yourself, what is the profile of employees that I want to hire? What kind of ethical behaviors that I expect from these employees? What is the level of motivation I expect from these employees? How will I attract them? What will I do to retain my employees so that they can give the best of themselves?

*- What are the opportunities for growth of your market?*

If you plan to start a business, you need to research the umbrella industry and find out what the opportunities for growth are. As said earlier, events in the financial and economic markets as well as current trends can help you understand the level of risk that you are about to take when starting your business. You need to answer clearly for yourself whether the market offers opportunities for the growth of your business.

*- What are the professional services that are available for your business? If you plan to use them, how and when do you plan to do that?*

As an entrepreneur, you may not have the necessary academic skills to write your business plan, design and set-up a data and financial management system, design marketing materials, or do other similar activities that require some expertise with respect to standards of quality for your business. Therefore, you may want to identify the professional services that you will need. Answer questions such as (a) "Where will I find them?", (b) "When will I use them?" (c) "What will that cost me?" (d) "What are the options of services available?"

*- What are specific manuals and guides that can help you better run your business?*

As a future business owner, you need to understand that the management of your resources will determine your success or your failure. For example, if you mismanage your money, neglect record keeping, develop bad relationships with employees and customers, you may find yourself in irreparable trouble, and get out of business. It is not a catastrophe if you don't have all the management skills that you need. However, you need to understand and acknowledge for yourself what you know and what you don't know, what you can do and what you cannot do. Identify people who can complete you. You may use task delegation strategies to get things done. In any case, you need to have an overview of what the tasks and indicators of quality completion are. You may learn some of that in workshops, seminars, or formal education courses. You will need to select some manuals or guides that you can refer to whenever it is necessary. These manuals or guides are part of resources that you may utilize.

*- What are the existing organizations or associations that can provide you with technical support for your business?*

In almost every city, there is at least one chamber of commerce or a nearby small business development center that can provide advice for small business start-up. There may be other city or county agencies, community colleges, colleges, universities, or non-profit organizations that may provide small business advice. Do your best to locate these organizations or associations where technical assistance for small business start-up is available. Contact them, and use their services as much as you can.

## Discover the proper attitudes

Attitude is the choice that we make to define and interpret our life experiences and respond to them. Much of what we think, value, believe, feel, expect, and do is related to our attitude. In fact, our attitude determines whether we will fail or succeed in an enterprise. During a research process to start a business, an entrepreneur must identify the proper attitudes of success that match with or complement his/her aptitudes to face identified challenges and better use available resources. The following questions can help define the attitudes that can help in starting and managing a business:

*- What is my start up sheet like?*

A start-up sheet is basically a draft document in which you consign all the tasks and expenses related to the starting of your business. A start-up sheet says a lot about your attitude. For example, the fact that you draft a start-up sheet indicates that you don't want to just think or talk about a business, but you actually take one of the first steps toward the concretization of your dream or vision.

*- What are the business ethical principles that I will be living by?*

Many corporations such as World Com, Enron, Parmalat failed because of poor or lack of ethical business practices. It does not matter how successful a business seem to be, if there are no ethical boundaries, the business will be gone sooner or later. You must list the basic ethical principles that your business will be living by. For example, you cannot sell defect products or provide a service of lower quality just to make more profit. If you are not sure about the safety of a product, you should not sell it. The manufacturer must provide that guarantee. If you make a mistake it has to be because the manufacturer misled you. Will you fire an employee just because he/she disagrees with you? These are some among the ethical questions that you will need to answer for yourself, your employees, partners, and customers.

*- What type of relationships I plan to develop with my employees (if any)?*

The nature of relationships between employer and employees can have positive or negative impact on the productivity of a business or the performance of the employees. If you treat your employees well, respect them, integrate them in the overall management of your business, give them a sense of ownership, there is no doubt that you will see the effect on your profit. However, if you treat them unfairly, your company will pay the price, and you might not even be able to notice that until you go out of business. It is important that an entrepreneur define the type of relationships that he/she plans to develop with the employees.

*- What are my customer service, marketing, and advertising strategies?*

Customers are becoming more and more demanding. Businesses must do their best to meet or possibly exceed the expectations of their customers. This fact is reinforced by the fierce competition that new businesses have to face in order to survive. Before you make the final decision to start a new business, be mindful of the strategies that you will use to attract new customers and retain your current clientele.

*- What are my public relations networking and outreach strategies?*

Public relations are alternative strategies to do marketing for a small business. Professional marketing can be very expensive. Public relations provide the opportunity to spend less while entertaining the possibility of being as effective as marketing. An entrepreneur should never miss the opportunity to use public relations as a tool to promote his/her business, attract new clients, and retain existing clients.

*- What are my daily, weekly, and monthly management strategies?*

The daily, weekly, and monthly management strategies constitute essentially the soul of a small business. They include the interactions with employees, clients, and partners, as well as the financial management, the record keeping and the provision of quality services. How do you plan to manage on daily, weekly, and monthly bases? The answers to this question can help someone hypothesize whether your business will succeed or not.

*- What are my strategies of evaluation?*

Even with the most careful planning, no one can predict what the future will bring with accuracy. Planning enhances the probability of better outcomes, but does not protect against unforeseen or unavoidable events. Planning does not exclude either the necessity for eventual adjustments. Given the possibility to deviate from the plan, it is imperative to assess whether a plan is being implemented properly. If yes, what part in the plan can be perfected? If no, what are the challenges? What are the needed adjustments?

*- What is my calendar of evaluation?*

Evaluation is not just an exercise. It carries a fundamental purpose of helping make better administrative and management decisions. An entrepreneur must know how often he/she plan to evaluate the achievement of goals and objectives?

*- What leadership styles or approaches can help you better run your business?*

There is a variety of leadership styles. An entrepreneur must read about the leadership styles in order to make self-assessment and understand which styles better fit his/her business needs. For example, the autocratic leader tends to believe that the best way to make people do what the leader wants is to have absolute control of the power to make decisions. Also, there is the democratic leader who incorporates the personalities, needs, wants, and drives of the people by creating a climate where individuals feel valued and respected as human being, not machines. Another type that I can mention is the laissez-faire leader who abstains from making any tough decision, and lets people do whatever pleases them. More importantly, you need to remember some of the common characteristics of leaders such as adaptability, alertness, communication skills, creativity, enthusiasm, flexibility, listening skills, open-mindedness, patience, resourcefulness, risk-taker, self-confidence, supportiveness, and teaching ability. The questions are (a) what leadership styles can help you better run your business? (b) What leadership characteristics do you strongly believe you have? (c) How do you plan to fill the gap, if any?

## Step forward!

You may go to a public or university library or use any documentation strategy of your choice during your research process to start your business. You may need to answer each question independently. Of course, the answer to each question is related to at least one other question. Once you can provide the appropriate answers to your research questions, you are ready to express your research in an organized manner, through a document that most scholars call a business plan.

**DO IT YOURSELF!**

1. Make a list of anticipated challenges for your business. Why do you consider them as challenges? What are the planned responses to each challenge?

2. Make a list of your personal aptitudes based on your past and present experiences. How do you plan to use them in your business?

3. Make a list of resources that are available for your business. What are the requirements to use them? How do you plan to use them as short-term, mid-term, or long-term opportunities for your business?

4. Make a list of ethical, leadership, managerial, and interpersonal attitudes that you intend to adopt to succeed in your business. Anticipate at least three situations in which you plan to use each of them.

5. The Rod Mendell case

Rod Mendell is a water sewer supervisor in Akron, Ohio. He has a total of 10 employees working under his supervision. Over the years, Rod has become a community leader in Akron. He is a board member in many community associations. He is a natural counselor for many community members. People who want to organize a community event would come to consult with him most of the time. His friends said that he is a very approachable and likeable individual. His supervisors and co-workers have testified in several occasions about his leadership abilities and work ethic.

Rod is planning to retire within three years. He is entertaining the idea of starting a small business. He has some concerns, because the State has been through a severe financial crisis. Many small businesses have either laid off most of their employees or shut their doors. Rod used a template provided by his friend and developed the following personal balance sheet:

Assets:

Financial assets
    Checking account        $ 7,200
    Saving account         $ 8,000
    IRA        $ 5,000
    Cash value of life insurance        $ 6,000
    Mutual fund shares        $ 3,400
    Total financial assets        $ 25,600

Nonfinancial assets:
    Home        $ 130,000
    Automobile        $ 16,000
    Furniture and appliances        $ 8,000
    Collectibles        $ 3,000
    Jewelry        $ 2,700
    Clothing        $ 3,000
    Books        $ 400

    Total nonfinancial assets        $ 163,100
    Total assets        $ 188,700

Liabilities and Net Worth

Short-term liabilities:
    Utility bills        $ 300
    Medical bills        $ 400
    Charge account balances        $ 1,600
    Furniture and appliances        $ 4,000

    Total short-term liabilities        $ 6,300

Long-term liabilities:
    Home mortgage        $ 110,000

Total liabilities        $ 116,300

Net Worth        $ 72, 400

Total liabilities and net worth        $188,700

Rod has an annual salary of $56,000. His net monthly income after all deductions is $3,720.00. He anticipates to receive a $ 1,000 bonus by the end of the year.

## Questions

1. What are the challenges faced by Rod to start a small business?

2. How do you think he could address these anticipated challenges?

3. What personal aptitudes do you think Rod can use in running a potential small business?

4. What are the resources that are available for Rod to start a small business? Explain how sustainable these resources are in your judgment!

5. What are the attitudes that you think Rod has to help him manage a small business?

6. Overall, would you recommend Rod to explore further the idea of starting a small business? Why?

7. Rod is not clear about what type of business to start, if any. What would you advise him to do? Or, what types of questions would you recommend Rod to ask to himself?

# Chapter III
## Expressing

The research process for an entrepreneur is basically a collection of facts, data, or evidence to show that the business an individual is dreaming about is worth being started. It also means that the facts and data must be expressed in a coherent and meaningful document, which is the business plan. The expressing phase means that you must indicate in a document that you are serious about business. Expressing means that you do not intend to travel in a blind adventure without any road map. Expressing means that you are capable of showing an eventual lender that you are a professional, and your business has the viability and ability to repay a loan. In other words, you must be able to argue an earning power. Let's see what a business plan is like.

### Starting a business means getting organized

Starting a business means getting organized. I mean time, money, materials, and relationship management. If you want to really organize yourself to start a business, you must be able to endure some sacrifices. You will have to work extra hours in addition to your regular work schedule. Your work day may become longer than that of your family members and your friends. You may have to spend less time with your family, hopefully for a short period of time. You will find less time for non-purposive conversations with your friends. Take the time to let them know that there is a modification in your schedule that may affect the frequency of your contacts so they know you are still available in case of emergency, even if they do not hear from you as frequently as they used to be. At this stage, there are two words that can be your companion for a long way: priority and time. You must set priorities and benchmarks if you want to complete efficiently the tasks toward the achievement of your goals. Setting priority is not enough without a good use of time management principles. Do not get trapped into the temptation to complete unplanned tasks that can wait until you are done with your task list. This is not a role of thumb. There may be time when you have to put your priorities aside to deal with an emergency. However, emergencies cannot occur daily. If an issue occurs on a regular basis as an emergency, I am almost certain that such emergency is not a real one. Think about how you can handle this situation in a more systematic way. You can, for example, include that issue in your regular planning. This strategy will enable you to be more effective.

## The need for a business plan

As I have already said, a business plan is a must for an entrepreneur who wants to succeed. Of course some people start their business without having a business plan. Consequently you might not hear from the majority of such businesses after four or five years. A business that comes from a dream and a research process cannot be a planned failure. It has to succeed. The business plan provides an entrepreneur this opportunity to put in writing where he/she is, where she/he wants to be or will be in the future, what she/he is going to do to get there, and how she/he will know when she/he gets there. You can understand that the business plan is a vital document. You can either seek professional assistance or do it yourself.

## Seek professional assistance

If you do not have all the skills and experience to write a business plan, you may consider hiring a professional to write one for you. However, this does not change anything in the process. I mean, do not ask a professional to write a business plan for you. You need to participate in the process of elaborating the document so you know clearly what it is about. Some entrepreneurs try to take some free advice from a consultant and attempt to put something together. It is a wrong and unethical practice. If you cannot write a document of business plan, let a professional do it. Keep in mind that you have to pay a professional for a professional document. If you do not value the service of a consultant, how can you expect that people value the products or services that you will sell in your business? This has been a source of failure for many entrepreneurs. Do not try to get free service from the service that a professional is selling, unless the person offers you to do so. If you write a mediocre business plan, it will not serve you to do too much. Actually, even if you hire a consultant, you still need to know what a business plan is like so you can better appreciate one that a consultant wrote for you.

## Do It Yourself

You may want to write the business plan yourself. There is no problem at all to do that, as long as you consent to spend the necessary time to write it. In fact, if you have the answers for all the questions in the preceding chapter, you have your business plan in hands. I mean, all the ideas are there. You just need to organize them into a coherent document. The following section of this chapter suggests an outline to write a business plan. There is a variety of formats to present a business. The content will vary with the requirements of your lender. If you are writing a business plan for your personal use, I would suggest the following template, which you can adjust (complement) to your situation.

## Components of a business plan

A business plan is a document that provides an entrepreneur systematic guidelines to operate a business. A business plan can be written for a start-up or an existing business. There is of course a difference between a business plan for a start-up business and one for an existing business.

A business plan for a start-up business draws the initial stages and projections about the operation of the business. On the other hand, a business plan for an existing business stresses the strategic direction that such a business intends to take based on existing and future conditions. The information in such a business plan is a better reflection of the reality of an existing business and the vision set for the future. The template suggested in this text deals primarily with the reality of a start-up business. A typical business plan includes:

- Cover letter (Optional)
- Non-Disclosure Statement
- Cover sheet
- Table of contents
- Business identification
- Executive summary
- Vision-Mission-Goals-Objectives
- Description or profile of the business
- Description of product(s)/ Service(s)
- Market analysis
- Competitive situation
- Marketing and sales strategies
- Operations management
- Action plan
- Financial framework
- Appendices

Here is an overview of the meaning of the items in the proposed outline:

## Cover letter (Optional)

Although the cover letter is optional, I believe that an entrepreneur should make it mandatory. The cover letter must inform clearly about:

- The name of your business,
- A summary of your vision and mission,
- The exact amount that you are requesting,
- The goal that this fund will help you attain.

## Non-Disclosure Statement

A well-written business plan is a potential fortune. It is an outcome of imagination, time, and money. You cannot just send it away and have other people use it for their own purpose. Like any document, you can copy right your business plan to protect your ownership.

Also, before you send out your business plan to people that are interested in investing in your business, it is good to have them sign a "Non-disclosure Statement". By signing a "Non-disclosure statement", they commit to keep confidential the information in your business plan.

## Cover sheet

The cover sheet includes the following information:
- The name of the business,
- The indication "BUSINESS PLAN",
- The date,
- The person contact (name, title, address, telephone, fax, email)
- The indication "Confidential document"

## Table of contents

Like in many other documents, the table of contents presents the chapters, sections, or sub-sections of the business plan, and the page numbers to find them.

## Business Identification

The business identification section presents:
- The name of the business,
- The business EIN (Employer Identification Number)
- The business address, telephone, and fax,
- Owners of the business and contact addresses
- Possibly other people involved in the business (Accountant, Attorney, Insurance…) and their addresses.

# Executive summary

The executive summary is an overview of the business. It includes the vision and the mission of your company, the goal (s) and objectives that you are pursuing, the strategies and capitalization that will help you attain them, and the potential capability of the business to make profit and repay a loan.

The executive summary may be no more than one page. Write the executive summary after you have completely written the business plan. It comes in the beginning of the document, but it must be a synthesis of what you have already written. Here is a sample of executive summary:

> Paradiz Childcare is an early childhood development corporation managed by a team of qualified and experienced professionals in early childhood education management, human services, and social work. The vision of Paradiz childcare is to be a leading early childhood development provider, which inspires confidence and trust of parents, families, and surrounding communities.
>
> All teachers and teacher-assistants will be certified and will have at least 5 years of experience in the field. The Paradiz childcare curriculum will include content areas, strategies, and activities similar to most Montessori preschools and schools.
>
> Paradiz Childcare Corporation commits to the highest quality of child care and early childhood education management. A center director and an assistant director will manage the day-to-day operations of the business, oversee staff, and ensure continuing evaluation for on-going quality improvement and the success of the business venture.
>
> The initial cost for start-up assets, legal compliances, advertising, facilities, equipment, and other related expenses is estimated to $60,000. Owners will contribute personal funds totaling $ 30,000, and a 5-year loan of

$30,000 will be sought. The industry analysis as well as the opportunity offered by the market provide substantial evidence of the potential to expand the daycare capacity up to 200% by the third year of operation, generate a return on investment (ROI) of 15% during the first year, increase sales of services to more than $1,000,000 by the third year, and bring gross margin up to above 25%, by the third year. Paradiz Child Care will be propelled into a suitable financial position within five years so it can initiate profitable acquisition.

## Vision-Mission-Goals-Objectives

In the first chapter, we have already defined what are vision, mission, goals, and objectives. The following are examples of vision, mission, goals, and objectives:

> **Vision:** The vision of Paradiz childcare is to be a leading early childhood development provider, which inspires confidence and trust of parents, families and surrounding communities.

> **Mission:** The mission of Paradiz childcare is to provide children a safe, secure, convenient, and nurturing child care environment, which will prepare children them for effective learning experience at school.

### Goals:
1. Offer advanced technology programs, after-school tutoring, and activities such as arts and crafts, dance, theatre and gymnastics.
2. Provide opportunities for children to develop self help skills and independence.
3. Assist children to develop communication skills and have the opportunity to express themselves through music and art.

4. Assist intellectual development, problem - solving, decision making and reasoning in children of all ages.
5. Encourage children to respect others' ideas, feelings, culture and property.
6. Encourage children to interact positively with peers and adults.
7. Help children gain self control and take responsibility for personal behavior.

**Objectives**
1. Open for daycare services 7 days a week by fall 200x.
2. Expand the daycare capacity up to 200% by the third year of operation.
3. Generate a return on investment (ROI) of 15% during the first year.
4. Increase sales of services to more than $1,000,000 by the third year.
5. Bring gross margin up to above 25%, by the third year.

# Description or profile of the business

The description or profile of your company is important to help a lender understand some factors that may affect your business. In the description you should specify:

- Whether you are a sole proprietorship or incorporation, or a limited liability company, or other;
- The precise nature of your business;
- Whether this is a new business or the purchase of an existing business, or a franchise, or other;
- Whether it is a seasonal or year-round business;
- Whether you have any contract or agreement or not;
- Your vendors, suppliers, outside contractors (if any);
- Your operational procedures;
- The local and national economic trends that influence your business, and how you will deal with them;
- And any other relevant information that can help better understand the profile of your business.

The following is an example of "Description or profile of the business".

> Paradiz childcare is a privately-held C-corporation owned in majority by its founders Peter Lester, Lesa Elder, Marc Peers, Sam Dobb, Sen Gue, and Holmer Ed. No one owns more than 25%, but all six owners are active participants in management decisions. Paradiz childcare will open for business on August 15, 201x. We anticipate starting with 100 children, and expect to nearly triple by the end of 201x.

We have already secured a suitable 4,000 sq.ft building located at 2270 Court Street, Tampa, FL 33617. The monthly leasing cost is $3,500.00. There used to be a child care at the facility. The former occupants of the building had recently relocated to their own facilities. There is basically no need for major renovation in the interior of the building. The Hillsborough County Early Childhood licensing agency, the health service department, and the fire and safety department have all approved the building as suitable to open a child care business. We have already completed the minor changes that they recommended in order to have more than the 80 parking lots currently available. The yard is fully fenced, and is furnished with safe and entertaining toys as well as sandbox.

## Description of Product(s)/ Service(s)

In this section you may explain in a clear and concise manner all relevant information about your products or services. Your lender does not have to guess what your business offers. Explain what makes your product or service unique, the tests or approvals that they passed, and the guaranty that you provide. Here is an example of description of products or services:

> Joy Child Care provides 24/7 child care services for ages from 3-month infants to 6 years old. Also, the center will offer pre- and after- school services for children from 6 to

12 years old. Pre- and after-school services will be offered Monday to Friday, from 6:00 am to 8:00 am and from 2:00 pm to 6:00 pm. Joy will help children learn through age appropriate activities, and will serve them nutritious meals and snack.

Joy facility is licensed to receive 300 children from ages two weeks to thirteen years. Joy has met the child to staff ratio and square footage required by licensing agencies in Kings County, New York. The teaching, support, administrative and auxiliary spaces are adjusted to the standards of high quality child care center. Each room includes appropriate storage to stock products that children do not need to be in contact with. The facility also has large outdoor storage capacity. We will ensure that the toys and equipment purchased for children are appropriate in the light of the Child Protection and Toy Safety Act. The facility provides special accommodation for children with disabilities.

Joy strives to encourage creativity by providing an environment filled with love, kindness and patience. Particular emphasis will be put on sensory and language development activities as well as math, science, housekeeping, and daily life skills. Parents will be involved to help children achieve weekly learning goals, and will be invited to participate in the childcare classroom activities.

## Competitive Situation

As an entrepreneur, you need to include in your business plan the local and national trends that may affect your business. You also need to provide the answers as to how you plan to address the anticipated competitive trends. Here is what the competitive situation will look like:

A childcare service is a multibillion – dollar industry. As a labor intensive industry, labor costs account for more than 50% of a childcare center total expenses. The total expended costs tend to decline proportionally to the increase of the number of children served. According to the Census Bureau's Report, a center with 50 or more full-time children realize up to 15% savings in total cost per child per hour. The percentage of cost savings is exponential to the increase of the number of children served. For example, a center with 100 children or more may realize a 30% cost savings.

In addition, the Census Bureau's Report projects that, within the next 10 years, the service sector will have the highest and fastest growing percentage of shift workers (45%) during non-standard hours. The report indicates that 15 million mothers with children under age 5 have the highest percentage of voluntary non-standard hours. Also, there will be a significant increase in percentage of employment positions requiring non-standard hours, such as doctors, nurses, and hotel and restaurant workers.

Childcare service is among the most underpaid industries. Childcare workers received fewer benefits and lower wages compared to other service industries. The employer turn-over tends to be higher, and consequently affects the quality of services offered to clients. Therefore, a sustainable childcare center should provide adequate wages and satisfactory benefits to its employees, in order to ensure the retention of highly qualified employees and guarantee higher quality services to children and parents.

## Market analysis

The market analysis section elaborates on the demographic, economic, and social profiles of the clients that are most in need of your products or services. This includes the identification of all your competitors, their strengths and weaknesses, and how you plan to compete with them. Here is an example of market analysis:

Rainbow child care intends to create a stable base of full-time clients, which ensure consistent revenue generation for an effective and profitable operation of the business. Management and staff will strive to use the highest standards in early childhood management and customer services to ensure that children are taken care of professionally at all times. Thus, Rainbow child care will keep the parents involved and highly satisfied so they maintain their children with us.

A 200x needs assessment conducted by the HOPE Foundation suggests that some parents or guardians have a need for part-time or drop-in child care services, based on special circumstances or emergency situations. Rainbow child care will use this opportunity to generate additional income by making flexible part-time services available.

Recent community needs assessments published by the Children's Services Commission of Hillsborough County indicated that there is an increase in the number of families that are in need of daycare and child care services during non-standard hours (after 6:00 pm). Separation and divorce have left many parents single while they have to work to provide for their children. There are also guardians who have parenting responsibilities while they have to work during non-standard hours.

More and more middle class couples work extra hours to cope with economic hardship or more demanding standard of living that connect directly with their family stability. There are over 200 child care centers in Hillsborough County. However, most facilities operate from 6:00 am to 6:00 pm. There are just a few facilities that provide 24/7 child care services. The business journal suggests that 24/7 child care business is one of the most stable industries in Hillsborough County. There is no evidence that this trend will change in the near future.

Undoubtedly, there is a potential market for high quality 24/7 child care services.

The Tampa Chamber of Commerce indicates that the child care business is very lucrative. Consequently, many corporations and individuals have been proactive in opening child care facilities to take advantage of this market. There are commercially-run centers such as KinderCare and Village care, and lots of individual-owned centers. The commercially-owned centers have built their reputations over time, and possess a stable client base. The individually-owned centers will be our main competitors in the beginning, because they offer services targeting the needs of our potential clients. However, according to the Consumer Watch Association, the quality of services offered by individually-owned child care centers in Hillsborough County is relatively poor. To keep the challenge with the immediate competitors, Rainbow child care will provide quality services that are competitive with the commercially-owned centers while maintaining lower staff to child ratio and lower fees. This will ensure competitiveness with both commercially-run and individually-owned child care centers. Rainbow child care plans to partner with community colleges, colleges, and universities in the Tampa Bay area, in order to use the internship opportunities of their early childhood education programs. This will enable us to offset certain costs.

## Marketing and sales strategies

This section concerns the marketing and sales strategies that you intend to implement in order to reach your clients or customers. The following is an example of market and sales strategies:

Paradiz plans to provide services within the 20 mile radius of Temple Terrace, Florida. Paradiz will offer flexible full-time and part-time options as well as special packages to parents based on their circumstances.

Potential clients for the business are:
- Friends living in surrounding neighborhoods,
- Members of local churches, clubs and organizations,
- Employees of public and private agencies in Hillsborough County, Florida,
- Employees of hospitals, nursing homes and assisted living facilities,
- Other service workers and professionals who have custody of children as parents or guardians.

Based on existing statistics for Hillsborough County, potential clients will have the following profiles:
- Typically: couple families, guardians, single parents.
- Age: 18 – 55 years old
- Education: Mainly college educated
- Household income: $ 40,000 – $100, 000
- Occupations: Hold services or professional jobs
- Socialization: Many belong to a club, an association or a local church
- Commute in their car
- Read newspapers and flyers
- Work during standard and non-standard hours
- Have concerned for quality care, affordability, and safety.

The Standard Industrial Classification (SIC) Code 8351 does not differentiate between family child care, preschool, nursery school, and child development centers. The following table indicates the number of child care facilities for the 5 closest zip codes:
- 33617 : 40 facilities
- 33612 : 54 facilities
- 33610 : 65 facilities
- 33613 : 70 facilities
- 33604 : 43 facilities

According to the 200x Hillsborough County

Neighborhood Report, the five closest zip codes will have 34,000 children between the ages of 0 to 4 in 2010. The median household income is $40,000, which is $ 5,000 more than the $35,000 national median household income.

Several contacts have been established with church leaders and members of neighborhood associations, which have already begun promotion by word of mouth. Response has been favorable. Formal advertising is planned to begin three months before the center is scheduled to open. Paradiz will be promoted in various local media. The print advertising will be placed in four local newspapers announcing the opening of the daycare. A member of a local newspaper offered the opportunity for a Business Brief article that will not cost any money. We plan to have the article to be printed before the open house, in order to facilitate pre-enrollment.

A poster and flyer will be developed and placed in all identified public facilities where they can be seen by our potential clients. We will seek to place notice in local church Sunday bulletins. An open house will be held to introduce the center. Throughout the year, Paradiz will have special and multicultural events for parents of children attending the center as well as members of the local communities. Local media will be contacted to cover the events. Also, the center will sponsor local cultural and sports events that target children and families.

Furthermore, full-time enrollees will receive 10% discount on full-time enrollment for each child after the first child. Parents who bring a new full-time client will receive a $20 gift card once the enrollment process is completed.

# Operations management

In the operations management section you describe the administration and the conduct of regular activities related to running your business. It also includes the people involved in decision making and implementation process of production or service delivery. Here is an example of how the operations management section may be written:

> The board of directors, which includes an executive director, will oversee the overall activities of the center. In addition, an advisory board will be created with parents and members of the local community. The advisory board will provide insight and advice to the board of directors and the management team of the center. The executive director will be responsible for the daily management of the center, and will have regular meetings with internal and external stakeholders, especially to discuss the operational and financial matters.
>
> A consultant computer analyst has already developed a computer program to manage students' and personnel records, track attendance, payment and expenditures. Financial data in the system are exportable to QuickBooks for accounting and reporting purposes.
>
> The daily operations of Paradiz Child Care will be managed by the following staff:

*Center Director:*
  The Center Director, Mark Page, will manage and coordinate the day-to-day operations of the center as well as the oversight of curriculum and activities of all instructors, caregivers and tutors. The following outlines Mark Page is qualifications and experience:
  • M.S. Degree in Early childhood Education
  • 5 years facilities administration/support experience with the Early Childhood Management of Queens, New York
  • 10+ years managerial/supervisory experience

*Financial Coordinator:*

The financial coordinator will:

- Process all receipts and disbursements.
- Process the payroll, including payroll tax returns.
- Submit requests for inter-fund transfers.
- Maintain and reconcile the general ledger monthly.
- With the center director, develop the annual budget.
- Prepare all financial reports, including requests for reimbursements.
- Manage the petty cash fund.
- Reconcile the bank accounts.
- Reconcile the statement of credit card deposits and service charges.
- Double check all reimbursement requests against receipts provided.

*Office Assistant*:

- Receives and opens all incoming mail, except the bank statements.
- Prepares cash receipts log and invoice log.

*Teacher*

The teacher will:

- Assess the needs of the students and establish objectives that are consistent with the center philosophy,
- Plan and implement activities throughout the day,
- Take daily attendance,
- Collaborate with staff, teacher assistants, and parents,

*Teacher Assistant*

- Assists the teacher in all activities,
- Participates in staff meetings,
- Takes daily attendance,
- Serves in other capacity as assigned by teachers.

Full-time and part-time children will be required to complete all necessary health, immunization, and

enrollment forms. The following fees will be charged for
attending Paradiz Childcare:

*For full-time weekly rates, 35 hours or more*
- Infants (6 weeks to 18 months) : $150
- Toddlers 18 moth to 2 ½ years) : $140
- Preschool (2 ½ to 4 years) : $130
- Before and after school (5–13 years): $120

*For Part-time weekly rates – up to 35 hours*
- Infants (6 weeks to 18 months) : $75
- Toddlers (18 moth to 2 ½ years) : $70
- Preschool (2 ½ to 4 years) : $65
- Before and after school (5–13 years): $60

## Action plan

The action plan details the steps or benchmarks that will help you
implement your business plan. The following table is an example of
action plan.

**Figure 2**
**Sample Start-up Business Action plan**

| Milestone | Start Date | End Date | Budget | Person Responsible |
|---|---|---|---|---|
| Signing lease | 08/01/200x | 09/30/200y | $ 5,000 | Owner |
| Purchasing materials and equipments | 07/15/200x | 07/30/200y | $ 5,000 | Center Director |
| Issuing job posting | 08/1/200x | 09/15/200y | $ 300 | Financial Coordinator |
| Hiring personnel | 09/15/200x | 10/01/200y | $ 500 | Center Director |
| Setting up curriculum | 10/01/200x | 10/30/200y | $ 1,000 | Center Director |
| Finalizing certification and licensing | 10/15/200x | 10/30/200y | $ 500 | Owner/ Center Director |
| Organizing outreach activities | 10/01/200x | 10/30/200y | $ 500 | Center Director |
| Organizing open house events | 10/1/2002 | 12/31/200y | $ 500 | Administrative Assistant |
| Starting services | 9/20/2002 | 12/31/200y | $ 3,000 | Center Director |

## Financial framework

The financial framework is, perhaps after the goals and objectives, the most important section in your business plan. A potential lender will pay a lot of attention to your financial framework. The financial framework includes your:

- Capital requirements,
- Depreciable assets
- Sales forecast
- Pro-forma Balance Sheet
- Projected income statements,
- Cash flow projections and analysis,
- And break-even analysis

*Capital requirements*

The capital requirements concern the money you need to start your business. This is basically your budget of investment. Your capital requirements include all your start up expenses and your working capital. The following is an example of capital requirements information:

**Figure 3**
**Sample Start-up Business capital requirements**

| Items | Costs (in Us $) |
|---|---|
| Requirements | |
| Start-up Expenses | |
| Legal fees | 2,000 |
| Rent/lease | 18,000 |
| Advertizing/Public relations | 1,000 |
| Furniture | 3,000 |
| Kitchen supplies | 2,000 |
| Naptime bedding | 1,000 |
| Cleaning supplies | 500 |
| Activity supplies | 1,000 |
| Stationery | 600 |
| First aid supplies | 400 |
| Other | 1,500 |
| Total start-up expenses | 30,000 |
| Start-up assets | |
| Cash balance starting date | 30,000 |
| Other current assets | 0 |
| Total current assets | 30,000 |
| Long-term assets | 0 |
| Total assets | 30,000 |
| Total requirements | 60,000 |

*Depreciable assets*

Depreciable assets are all assets of your business that depreciate over a period of time. For example, when you purchase a vehicle or equipment, you have a depreciable asset that helps you run your business. There is an initial cost for such asset, which is the price of purchase. But, once you start using this asset, it loses some value until it becomes useless. **This deterioration in value of an asset (real estate may go up in value) is called depreciation**. In accounting, depreciation is considered as an expense. The most common depreciation method is called straight-line depreciation. It consists of:

- identifying the initial cost of the asset,
- estimating for how many years you think such asset will have some value for your business,
- dividing the initial cost by the number of years.

In other words,

Depreciation=Initial cost ÷ Estimated asset lifetime

Here is an example of depreciation for a $20,000.00 copier machine:

### Figure 4
### Sample Straight-Line Depreciation

| Year | Straight-Line Depreciation | |
| --- | --- | --- |
| | Book Value | Annual Depreciation |
| Starting | $20,000 | $ - |
| First | 18,000 | 2,000 |
| Second | 16,000 | 2,000 |
| Third | 14,000 | 2,000 |
| Fourth | 12,000 | 2,000 |
| Fifth | 10,000 | 2,000 |
| Sixth | 8,000 | 2,000 |
| Seventh | 6,000 | 2,000 |
| Eight | 4,000 | 2,000 |
| Ninth | 2,000 | 2,000 |
| Tenth | | 2,000 |
| Eleventh | | |
| Twelfth | | |
| | | 20,000 |

## Sales Forecast

Sales forecasting is the process of estimating sales volume, expenses, and projected profits for the first or five years of a business. Here is a sample of sales forecast:

## Figure 5
## Sample Sales Forecast

| Sales Forecast | | | |
|---|---|---|---|
| | Year1 | Year2 | Year3 |
| Unit Sales | | | |
| Full-time Couples | 100 | 300 | 600 |
| After School Care | 100 | 200 | 300 |
| Summer Camp | 50 | 60 | 70 |
| Part-time Workers/Drop-Ins | 40 | 50 | 60 |
| Total Unit Sales | 290 | 610 | 1030 |
| | | | |
| Unit Prices | 2003 | 2004 | 2005 |
| Full-time Couples | $480.00 | $480.00 | $480.00 |
| After School Care | $210.00 | $210.00 | $210.00 |
| Summer Camp | $480.00 | $480.00 | $480.00 |
| Part-time Workers/Drop-Ins | $100.00 | $100.00 | $100.00 |
| | | | |
| Sales | | | |
| Full-time Couples | $48,000.00 | $144,000.00 | $288,000.00 |
| After School Care | $21,000.00 | $42,000.00 | $63,000.00 |
| Summer Camp | $24,000.00 | $42,000.00 | $ 33,600.00 |
| Part-time Workers/Drop-Ins | $4,000.00 | $ 5,000.00 | $6,000.00 |
| Total Sales | $97,000.00 | $103,400.00 | $390,600.00 |
| | | | |
| Direct Unit Costs | 2003 | 2004 | 2005 |
| Full-time Couples | $12.00 | $14.00 | $16.00 |
| After School Care | $5.00 | $7.00 | $9.00 |
| Summer Camp | $13.00 | $15.00 | $17.00 |
| Part-time Workers/Drop-Ins | $0.00 | $0.00 | $0.00 |
| | | | |

| Direct Cost of Sales | | | |
|---|---|---|---|
| Full-time Couples | $1,200.00 | $4,200.00 | $9,600.00 |
| After School Care | $500.00 | $1,400.00 | $2,700.00 |
| Summer Camp | $650.00 | $900.00 | $1,190.00 |
| Part-time Workers/Drop-Ins | $0 | $0 | $0 |
| Subtotal Direct Cost of Sales | $2,350.00 | $6,500.00 | $13,490.00 |
| Gross Margin | $94,650.00 | $96,900.00 | $377,110.00 |
| Gross Margin % | 97.57% | 93.71% | 96.54% |
| Expenses | | | |
| Payroll | $60,000.00 | $62,000.00 | $80,000.00 |
| Sales and Marketing and Other Expenses | $1,000.00 | $1,200.00 | $2,000.00 |
| Depreciation | $0 | $0 | $0 |
| Rent | $24,000.00 | $24,000.00 | $24,000.00 |
| Utilities | $6,000.00 | $6,200.00 | $7,500 |
| Insurance | $3,000.00 | $3,200.00 | $4,000 |
| Payroll Taxes | $9,000.00 | $9,300.00 | $12,000.00 |
| Operating Expenses | $103,000.00 | $105,900.00 | $129,500.00 |
| Profit Before Interest and Taxes | ($8,350.00) | ($9,000.00) | $247,610.00 |
| Net Profit | ($8,350.00) | ($9,000.00) | $211,706.95 |
| Net Profit/Sales | -8.60% | 8.70% | 54.20% |

*Projected income statements or Profit and Loss Statement*

The projected income statement or profit and loss statement is an estimation of income and expenses of the business within a period of time, which can be three to five years. The projected income statement includes:

**Sales**: net sales in dollars (or currency).

**Direct Cost of Sales or Cost of goods sold**: Cost of products or services that you have sold.

**Gross margin or gross profit**: Sales less cost of goods sold

**Selling expenses**: Sales salaries, advertising, delivery expenses, bad debt expenses, credit card fees, and other similar selling expenses.

**Administrative expenses**: salaries, utilities, depreciation, rent, building services, insurance, utilities, phone, and other similar administrative expenses.

**Operating expenses**: costs of goods sold plus selling and administrative expenses.

**Profit before tax**: Sales less operating costs.

**EBITDA:** Earnings Before Interest, Tax, Depreciation and Amortization.

**Net profit**: Profit before taxes less taxes.

Here is a format of income statements (*The data are fictitious and do not reflect the reality of an existing company.*):

**Figure 6**
**Sample Pro Forma Profit and Loss**

| Pro Forma Profit and Loss | | | |
|---|---|---|---|
| | Year1 | Year2 | Year3 |
| Sales | $97,000.00 | $103,400.00 | $390,600.00 |
| Less: Cost of Sales | $2,350.00 | $6,500.00 | $13,490.00 |
| Gross Margin | $94,650.00 | $96,900.00 | $377,110.00 |
| Gross Margin % | 97.57% | 93.71% | 96.54% |
| Selling expenses | | | |
| Sales and Marketing and Other Expenses | $1,000.00 | $1,200.00 | $2,000.00 |
| Total selling expenses | $1,000.00 | $1,200.00 | $2,000.00 |
| | | | |
| Administrative Expenses | | | |
| Payroll | $60,000.00 | $62,000.00 | $80,000.00 |
| Depreciation | $0 | $0 | $0 |
| Rent | $24,000.00 | $24,000.00 | $24,000.00 |
| Utilities | $6,000.00 | $6,200.00 | $7,500 |
| Insurance | $3,000.00 | $3,200.00 | $4,000 |

| | | | |
|---|---|---|---|
| Payroll Taxes | $9,000.00 | $9,300.00 | $12,000.00 |
| Other | $0 | $0 | $0 |
| Total administrative expenses | $102,000.000 | $104,700.00 | $127,500.00 |
| | | | |
| Operating Expenses | $103,000.00 | $105,900.00 | $129,500.00 |
| | | | |
| Profit Before Interest and Taxes | ($8,350.00) | ($9,000.00) | $247,610.00 |
| EBITDA | ($8,350.00) | ($9,000.00) | $247,610.00 |
| Less taxes | $0 | $0 | $35,903.00 |
| | | | |
| Net Profit | ($8,350.00) | ($9,000.00) | $211,706.95 |
| Net Profit/Sales | -8.60% | 8.70% | 54.20% |

*Cash flow projections*

The cash flow projection displays in-flow and out-flows of cash in the business within a period of time, which can be 12 to 36 months or even more. The cash flow projection concerns the net income of the business. In other words, it deals only with actual cash transactions. It shows the amount of cash needed to operate the business over time and when there will be positive cash flow. The cash flow projection includes:

**Starting cash:** The amount of cash you start with.

**Cash disbursement**: Receivables from sales of products or service and possibly from other sources.

**Cash uses**: Includes costs of goods sold, operating expenses, income tax, etc.

**Ending cash**: Cash in hand at the end of the period. Except for the first month, the ending cash of a period is the starting cash for the following period. Here is a format of cash flow projection:

## Figure 7
## Sample Pro Forma Cash Flow

| Pro Forma Cash Flow | | | |
|---|---|---|---|
| | Year1 | Year2 | Year3 |
| Starting cash | | | |
| Cash Sales | $97,000.00 | $103,400.00 | $390,600.00 |
| Subtotal Cash from Operations | $97,000.00 | $103,400.00 | $390,600.00 |
| | | | |
| Additional Cash Received | | | |
| Sales Tax, VAT, HST/GST Received | $0 | $0 | $0 |
| New Current Borrowing | $0 | $0 | $0 |
| New Other Liabilities (interest-free) | $0 | $0 | $0 |
| New Long-term Liabilities | $0 | $0 | $0 |
| Sales of Other Current Assets | $0 | $0 | $0 |
| Sales of Long-term Assets | $0 | $0 | $0 |
| New Investment Received | $0 | $0 | $0 |
| Subtotal Cash Received | $97,000.00 | $103,400.00 | $390,600.00 |
| | | | |
| Expenditures | Year 1 | Year 2 | Year 3 |
| | | | |
| Expenditures from Operations | | | |
| Cash Spending | $60,000.00 | $62,000.00 | $80,000.00 |
| Bill Payments | $42,000.00 | $43,000.00 | $50,000.00 |
| Subtotal Spent on Operations | $102,000.00 | $105,000.00 | $130,000.00 |
| | | | |
| Additional Cash Spent | | | |
| Sales Tax, VAT, HST/GST Paid Out | $0 | $0 | $0 |

| | | | |
|---|---|---|---|
| Principal Repayment of Current Borrowing | $0 | $0 | $0 |
| Other Liabilities Principal Repayment | $0 | $0 | $0 |
| Long-term Liabilities Principal Repayment | $10,000.00 | $10,000.00 | $10,000.00 |
| Purchase Other Current Assets | $0 | $0 | $0 |
| Purchase Long-term Assets | $0 | $0 | $0 |
| Dividends | $0 | $0 | $0 |
| Cash uses | $112,000.00 | $115,000.00 | $140,000.00 |
| | | | |
| Ending cash | ($15,000.00) | $11,600.00 | $250,000.00 |

*Pro-forma Balance Sheet*

The pro-forma balance sheet is a projected balance sheet that shows the distribution of the assets, liabilities and equity of the business at a given point in time.

**Assets**: Include **current assets** (cash, accounts receivables, notes receivables, prepaid expenses, inventories, and any other item convertible in cash within one year in the normal course of business), **fixed assets or long term assets** (land, buildings, equipments, vehicles, leasehold improvement, machinery, and any other item with estimated useful life measured in years), and **other assets** (deposit on a franchise, pre-opening expenses, etc)

**Liabilities and owner's equity**: Include **current liabilities** (debts and obligations that will be paid within one year such as accounts payables, notes payables, taxes payables, salaries), **long term liabilities** (debts and obligations due in more than one year, such as mortgages, equipment loans, bank loans, etc), and **owner's equity** (initial investment, retained earnings, common stock, etc). Here is a standard format of a balance sheet:

# Projected Balance Sheet

The balance sheet in the following table shows managed but sufficient growth of net worth, and a gradually sufficient healthy financial position.

## Figure 8
## Sample Pro Forma Balance Sheet

| Pro Forma Balance Sheet | | | |
|---|---|---|---|
| | Year 1 | Year 2 | Year 3 |
| Assets | | | |
| Current Assets | | | |
| Cash | $60,000.00 | $90,000.00 | $100,000.00 |
| Other Current Assets | $20,000.00 | $20,000.00 | $25,000.00 |
| Total Current Assets | $80,000.00 | $110,000.00 | $135,000.00 |
| | | | |
| Long-term Assets | | | |
| Long-term Assets | $0 | $0 | $0 |
| Accumulated Depreciation | $0 | $0 | $0 |
| Total Long-term Assets | $0 | $0 | $0 |
| Total Assets | $80,000.00 | $110,000.00 | $135,000.00 |
| | | | |
| Liabilities and Owners' Equity | Year 1 | Year 2 | Year 3 |
| | | | |
| Current Liabilities | | | |
| Accounts Payable | $8,000.00 | $9,000.00 | $10,000.00 |
| Current Borrowing | $0 | $0 | $0 |
| Other Current Liabilities | $0 | $0 | $0 |
| Total Current Liabilities | $8,000.00 | $9,000.00 | $10,000.00 |
| | | | |

| | | | |
|---|---|---|---|
| Long-term Liabilities | $40,000.00 | $30,000.00 | $20,000.00 |
| Total Liabilities | $48,000.00 | $39,000.00 | $30,000.00 |
| | | | |
| Owners' Equity | | | |
| Common stock | $12,000.00 | $21,000.00 | $50,000.00 |
| Retained earnings | $20,000.00 | $50,000.00 | $65,000.00 |
| Total Equity | $32,000.00 | $71,000.00 | $115,000.00 |
| Total Liabilities and Equity | $80,000.00 | $110,000.00 | $135,000.00 |

*Break-even analysis*

Before making a profit, a business must be able to generate enough income to cover all expenses. The amount of money or the number of unit of product or service sold through which the total revenue equals the total expenses is called the "**break-even point**".

The operation of a business requires fixed and variable costs.

**Fixed costs** are those costs that remain constant regardless the volume of sales (rent, salaries, telephone)

**Variable costs** are the costs that vary with the volume of sales (costs of good sold, labor costs, commissions, etc)

The variable costs can help calculate the contribution margin (CM), which is the difference between unit sales costs (USC) and the unit variable costs (UVC). In other words,

$$CM = USC - UVC$$

The break-even point is obtained by dividing the total fixed costs (FC) by the contribution margin. In other words,

$$BE = FC / CM$$

For example, you plan to open a restaurant with 40 seats. The fixed costs are US$ 60,000 per year for utilities, insurance, and salaries. The variable costs are $6 per cover ($3 for food ingredients, $2 for labor, and $1 for overhead). You plan to charge $10 per cover.

The contribution margin is:

CM = USC - UVC

CM = $10 - $6

CM= $4

The break-even point will be:

BE = FC/CM

BE = $60,000/$4

BE=15,000 covers per year.

Then, the break-even point is 15,000 covers per year or 1,250 covers per month or 41, 66 covers per day. This is the number of covers that the restaurant must sell so that the revenue equals the expenses. The profit will come beyond this point.

The break-even can also be calculated according to the following:

- **Average per-unit revenue** = Total sales / Total unit sales.
- **Average Per-Unit Variable Cost** = Direct cost of sales / Total unit sales.
- **Estimated Monthly Fixed Cost** = Operating expenses/12.
- **Monthly Units Break-even** = Estimated monthly fixed cost / (Average per unit revenue – Average per unit variable cost).
- **Monthly Revenue Break-even** = Fixed cost + (variable costs x monthly unit break even).

Here is an example based on the following data:

Total sales: $97,000.00
Total unit sales: 290
Operating expenses: $103,000.00
Direct cost of sales: $2,350.00

**Figure 9**
**Sample Break-even Analysis**

| Break-even Analysis | |
|---|---:|
| Monthly Units Break-even | 27 |
| Monthly Revenue Break-even | $8,802.00 |
| *Assumptions:* | |
| Average Per-Unit Revenue | $334.50 |
| Average Per-Unit Variable Cost | $ 8.10 |
| Estimated Monthly Fixed Cost | $ 8,583.00 |

# Appendices

In appendices you add all relevant information or documents in support of your business. For example, you may include contracts, agreements, list of suppliers, patents or copyrights, legal documents, and any other document.

# It's time for action!

Whether you hired a consultant or decided to do it yourself, you have your document of business plan in hand. This is a great investment. You have overcome one of the strongest barriers that could hinder you from achieving your dream. It is now time for action!

## DO IT YOURSELF!

1. Choose a name for your business. What does this name mean for you? How do you think this name will attract people to do business with you?

2. Provide in three or four paragraphs an overview of a business that you would like to start.

3. Make a start-up cost for a business that you would like to start! Explain how you plan to get the money!

4. Create a sales forecast, income statement, and balance sheet for the first three years of your business. Calculate the monthly unit and revenue break-even points!

4.1. Sales forecast

## 4.2. Income statement

## 4.3. Balance sheet

## 4.4. Break-even points

5. The Denver T-Shirts case

Denver T-Shirt is a new small business that Fred is planning to start in Denver, Colorado. He plans to buy quality T-shirts at $3.00 a piece. He estimates that he will spend $4.00/T-shirt for overhead expenses. In addition, he will have to commit an annual $30,000 of fixed costs. Given these facts, he anticipates a selling price of $12.00 per T-shirt.

## Questions

1.  How many T-shirts that must be sold before the business start making a profit?
2.  One consultant advised Fred that he will be able to sell between 4,000 and 5,000 T-shirts per month. What would be your recommendation to Fred? Explain the recommendation.
3.  Given the quality of the T-shirts, the consultant suggests to raise the selling price to $15.00. Would you recommend Fred to start the business based on that scenario? Explain your recommendation!

6. The Joni and Mark Company (JMC) case

The Joni and Mark Company (JMC) is based in Atlanta, Georgia. The company collects used books and computers, resells them to make a profit. The balance on JMC accounts on June 1 of the current year were as follows:

Cash: $ 100,000
Supplies: $25,000
Equipment: $ 175,000
Account payable: $100,000
Capital: $200,000

The transactions during the month of June appear below.
Paid salaries for $90,000
Bought additional equipment on account for $50,000
Received payments from individuals for $45,000
Paid delivery expenses for $20,000
Received payments from ACRON Corporation for $85,000

Question

Prepare a balance sheet for the period ending June 30, 2007

7. NLF Community store is a retail store based in Madison, Wisconsin. The transactions during
the current year were as follows:

Credit sales: $ 4,000,000
Cash sales: $ 1,000,000
Cost of goods sold: $ 1,600,000
Selling, general, and administrative expenses: $ 550,000
Depreciation: $ 350,000
Interest: $ 300,000
Taxes on income: $ 300,000
Dividends on common stock: $200,000

### Question

Prepare an income statement based on the information provided.

# CHAPTER IV
## Acting

The best friends of your dream are your plan and actions. You have already made the planning step by expressing your ideas on paper. The other step is to act on it. Acting on your dream means its metamorphosis into reality. Acting means executing your action plan, complying with legal requirements, settling your business, outreaching, hiring your personnel, organizing your facilities, and opening sales activities.

## Implementation calendar

We have previously mentioned the need for a start up check list. The startup check list enlists all the activities that you have to do in order to start operating your business. You put a check mark after each activity on your check list that you have completed. We also said that starting a business means getting organized. More than ever before, it is time for the use of the start up check list and the application of the organized and disciplined spirit, through an implementation calendar.

What is an implementation calendar? An implementation calendar is a document detailing the activities that must be executed toward the opening of a business. It is inspired by your dream, your research process, and your business plan. The implementation calendar includes the questions "when?", "what?", "who?", "how?" More specifically it includes the starting dates, execution dates, activities, person in charge, the deadline for execution, and indicators of measurement.

**Figure 10**
**Implementation calendar Template**

Business Name
Implementation Calendar

| When | | What | Who? | How? |
|---|---|---|---|---|
| Starting date | Execution deadline | Activity | Person responsible | Indicator of measurement |
| 02/03/05 | 02/20/05 | Apply for fictitious name | Business owner | Certificate of fictitious name from the State. |
| | | | | |
| | | | | |
| | | | | |
| | | | | |
| | | | | |
| | | | | |

## Process evaluation Form

A process evaluation form helps you monitor your progress in your implementation calendar. You may have a good implementation calendar that remains a piece of paper. What makes it a living document is a process evaluation sheet. This will prevent you unavoidable surprises at the last minute, by making necessary adjustments in your implementation calendar. The process evaluation form includes the planned activity, the specification of achievement, and comments about an activity.

### Figure 11
### Process evaluation Template

Business Name
Process Evaluation Form

| Planned Activity | Completed Activity | | Indicator of measurement | Activity in Process | Deadline | Comments |
|---|---|---|---|---|---|---|
| | Yes | Date | | | | |
| Apply for fictitious name | X | 02/18/05 | Certificate of fictitious name is on file. | | | |
| | | | | | | |
| | | | | | | |
| | | | | | | |

## Legal compliance

I understand that in the research process you have identified the legal requirements that match the business you are starting. It is now time to take action and comply with the laws that regulate your business environment. For example, you will need to:

- Make the final decision on a name for your business,
- Draft and sign your partnership agreement, for partnership, Limited Liability Company, joint venture, trust, or cooperative.
- Apply for your fictitious name,
- File your paper of incorporation, if you chose to start a corporation,
- Write your bylaws, for a corporation,
- Apply for and obtain an Employer Identification Number (EIN) from the Internal Revenue Services (IRS),
- Apply for and obtain required county license(s),
- Apply for and obtain required city license(s),
- Comply with legal insurance requirements,
- Apply for and obtain other required permits for your business.

## Bank account

Once you have your legal documents, especially the legal documents from your State and your EIN (Employer Identification Number), you must open a business account with a bank or a credit union of your choice. Again, do your homework to see which bank offers you the best service at the lowest cost for your business. Do your homework to see which bank is most likely to give you a loan. Open your account there.

## Figure 12
## Bank comparative form

Business Name
Bank comparative Form

| Bank | Service fees | Special services not found elsewhere | Accessibility within "x" miles | | | Potentiality for loan | | |
|---|---|---|---|---|---|---|---|---|
| | | | Close | Average | Far | Low | Average | High |
| | | | | | | | | |
| | | | | | | | | |
| | | | | | | | | |

# Settlement

The settlement is the place where the business will conduct product or service sales operations. The entrepreneur must arrange the rent, lease or purchase of a physical location, the organization of the facility (ies) with necessary materials and equipment, and the hiring of employees (if any).

*Location*

As we have seen previously, the physical location is very critical for business. Even if you have the proper financial resources for your business, moving from one location to another soon after starting a business is very costly. You should avoid it, by taking the time to select where to locate your business. The demographics about your trading area must necessarily determine your choice of a location. In other words, you must carefully examine the age group of the population in the area where you are conducting business, their occupations, their level of income, education, the change in the population, the crime rate in the area, the level of occurrence of vehicle accidents in the surrounding areas. This is information that you can find, for example, on the web sites of the Standard Metropolitan Statistical Area, the Department of Motor Vehicle of your State, the local sheriff's office, the local police department, or the main Chamber of Commerce of your state.

In addition, when choosing a location, do not rush to sign a lease contract without professional advice. Compare different square foot costs. Find out about zoning requirements from the city or county office where you are starting your business. Make sure that the contract does not contain any clause that may eventually restrain the expansion of your business. If the landlord would like to facilitate you to some extent, make sure that everything is stated in the contract. If there is any repair or space reorganization, make sure it is clearly written in detail what needs to be done, who is responsible to do what, and when?

*Equipment*

When starting a business, you need equipment that can serve you as support to better deliver your product or service. By equipment, I mean not only equipment such as computer, printer, copier, fax, and phone, but also

- furniture (desks, chairs, tables, files, bookcases, wastebasket, storage cabinets, safe, etc),
- office supplies (computer disks and CDs, staplers, scissors, glue, paper clips, pens, pencils, markers, printer cartridges, note and message pads, stationery, software, etc),
- general supplies (artworks, whiteboards, coffeemaker and coffee, microwave, bathroom and cleaning supplies, etc),
- and all improvement needs in your facilities (painting, carpeting, additional electrical outlets, signage, cleaning, etc).

You may want to use this equipment acquisition form that I suggest.

### Figure 13
### Equipment acquisition form

Business Name
Equipment Acquisition Form

| Code/ Equipment | Potential providers | Address Telephone Email of providers | Anticipate purchase date | Purchase date | Exact cost | Mode of payment |
|---|---|---|---|---|---|---|
|  |  |  |  |  |  |  |
|  |  |  |  |  |  |  |
|  |  |  |  |  |  |  |
|  |  |  |  |  |  |  |
|  |  |  |  |  |  |  |

# Outreach

When you are in the acting stage of starting your business, outreach is a must. From this depends some of your most faithful clients. You may need to identify the neighborhood associations, local churches, chamber of commerce, and community events that you will present yourself and your business. You will need business cards, flyers, and brochures related to your business. If you can have sample of products, do not hesitate to let people see them. Also, you will have to articulate your outreach activities into your implementation calendar.

# Opening

An opening is an event that you can organize when your business starts to become operational. You invite people to come to celebrate with you. This is a public relations event that requires some planning. It should be an activity in your implementation calendar. An opening should be planned well in advance so the people you are inviting can make plan to attend. The first thing you will need to do is create an invitation list, decide on a proper venue, and an "Open House Task List", which indicates who is doing what? And when? In other words, you need to:

- specify the nature of the task in non-equivocal terms,
- the date the task must be completed,
- the primary responsible for the completion of this task,
- the person of support if needed or in case of an accident or unforeseen situation,
- the outcomes (what will provide evidence that the task was completed?).

Here an example of template for an "Open House Task List".

## Figure 14
## Open House Task List

| Task | Date | Primary responsible | Support responsible | Outcomes |
|------|------|---------------------|---------------------|----------|
|      |      |                     |                     |          |
|      |      |                     |                     |          |
|      |      |                     |                     |          |
|      |      |                     |                     |          |
|      |      |                     |                     |          |

## Customer service

In the acting phase you have to think seriously about customer services. Sooner or later you will have to deal with some customer service issues, which may define the future of your business. Successful businesses are generally customer-oriented. The thumb rule is: The customer is always right! This does not mean that you have to let customers abuse or ruin your business. On the contrary, this means you must find a way to always make your customers happy so they won't feel that it's okay to abuse your business as a form of retaliation against unsatisfactory services. When customers are happy with services provided by a business they come back, even when they have other options. When customers are not happy they come back only if they have no other choice.

## Marketing and advertising

In the business plan, you expressed how you planned to market your product or service and advertise your business. In the acting stage, you have to execute the activities that you planned to implement. You will have to tell your customers what makes your business different from other similar businesses, so they can use your products and services over these of your competitors. You can use less expensive strategies such as coupons in print advertising for your customers, gifts for a certain number of first come customers or for a certain amount of purchase. You can sponsor community events, organize contests, issue posters, and other strategies that you find effective. Also, you may invest in more expensive strategies such as radio, television, newspaper, and magazine advertising. However, the most effective advertising and marketing strategy that you can use is the outstanding service that you provide to your customers. It will give you incredible referrals, which can create a stable client base for your business.

## It's time for managing!

Actually, you are no longer in a dream. That yesterday dream becomes today reality. You are in business. You are about to face with many challenges to stay in business and to make it prosper. This is the challenge of management. It is time for managing!

## DO IT YOURSELF!

1. Create an implementation calendar to start your business.

2. Make a list of activities and materials to purchase in preparation for a business opening event. Indicate the costs for each activity or item to purchase, and who will be responsible for such activities.

3. Make a list of advertising and marketing strategies that you plan to use when you start your business. When do you plan to use each strategy? What is the cost for each advertising and/or marketing strategy?

4. What is the anticipated profile of your potential employees?

5. How can you convince yourself with measurable facts that you chose the best location possible for your business?

# CHAPTER V
## Managing Operations

M any people have tried to start a business. Some of them failed because they did not have any dream. They did not know what they wanted, or where they wanted to go. Some people started with a dream. They closed their business later or after a year. They failed to achieve their dream, maybe because they did not think it was necessary to research, express, and act on their dream the proper way. Some others failed despite of researching, expressing, and acting on their dream. They failed because most of the time they neglected one piece of the dream puzzle: the management piece. You can be a good planner. But if you do not take the appropriate time to make the right decisions and adjust yourself to the change in market and consumer behavior, your management experience can become a failure. Of course it is always possible to reorganize yourself as long as you can understand the message of your market. In fact, this is what management is there for.

Operations management is the first big challenge for a small business entrepreneur. Basically, operations management consists of planning, staffing, supervising, and evaluating daily activities so the business can perform productively and achieve its objectives, goals, mission, and vision. In other words, planning does not end with a business plan. This is an ongoing process of evaluation and decision making.

## Strategic Management and Planning

Strategic management is usually one of the activities that small business owners tend to neglect. But this is the strength of most big corporations. The lack of strategic planning can be very disastrous for a business whether it is small or large. We have already seen the importance of operational planning in operations management. But, operations management to a large extent depends on strategic management. Basically, you can design your strategic planning based on the screening of your vision, your mission, and the evaluation of the overall performance of your business. Then, by using the CARA approach or the SWOT analysis, you can define long term goals and objectives for your business, and the strategies to achieve them. You can effectively expand your business only through strategic management.

You already have a business plan. In the business plan you expressed how you were going to manage your business operations. Now, you have to narrow your plan into quarterly, monthly, weekly, and daily plans. When you are planning, involve your employees as much as possible. Make planning adjustments that show them you are serious about their participation in managing the business. Do not just invite them to participate and ignore their suggestions. Make them feel that they are valued contributors to the entire planning and implementation process of your activities.

## Quarterly Plan

Most companies have a quarterly planning session to assess progress, identify challenges and opportunities, in order to achieve broader strategic goals. A quarterly plan includes goal (s), objectives, activities or tasks to be completed, strategies of task completion, persons responsible, indicators of measurement, and deadline. The quarterly plan enables a small business owner to make necessary adjustments throughout the year.

## Figure 15
## Quarterly plan

Business Name
Period from_____ To_____

| Goal | Objectives | Activities | Strategies | Person Responsible | Indicators of measurement | Deadline | | | | |
|------|-----------|-----------|-----------|-------------------|--------------------------|----------|---|---|---|---|
| | | | | | | | | | | |

# Monthly Plan

The quarterly plan can be organized in three sequences of monthly plans. The monthly plan indicates the activities, strategies, person responsible, indicators of measurement, and deadline related to a particular month. Having monthly plans makes it easier to determine whether the quarterly plan is being effectively implemented.

**Figure 16**
**Monthly Plan**

Business Name
Period from_____ To_____

| Activity | Strategies | Person responsible | Indicator of measurement | Deadline |
|---|---|---|---|---|
|  |  |  |  |  |
|  |  |  |  |  |
|  |  |  |  |  |
|  |  |  |  |  |
|  |  |  |  |  |

# Weekly Plan

From the monthly plan, the manager of a small business can elaborate detailed weekly plans. The weekly plan outlines the activities, persons responsible, and indicators of measurement for each work day. This helps increase productivity and better monitor staff performance.

**Figure 17**
**Weekly plan**

Business Name
Period from_____ To_____

| Day | Activities | Person responsible | Indicator of measurement |
|---|---|---|---|
| | | | |
| | | | |
| | | | |
| | | | |
| | | | |
| | | | |

# Daily Plan

Employees cannot come to work and second guess what they will be doing. Likewise, they cannot do everything at the same time. The work day must be organized as efficiently as possible. The daily plan offers this opportunity. It helps a supervisor monitor the daily performance of the supervisees, and facilitate the employees to better value their time and productivity. The daily plan stresses activities to be completed, persons responsible, and indicators of measurement related to a shift day of work.

**Figure 18**
**Daily plan**

Business Name

Day_____ Shift_____

| Time | Activities | Person responsible | Indicator of measurement |
|------|-----------|--------------------|--------------------------|
|      |           |                    |                          |
|      |           |                    |                          |
|      |           |                    |                          |
|      |           |                    |                          |
|      |           |                    |                          |

## Sales records and Inventory

Good management of your business starts by setting sales goals, recording individual sales transactions, and summarizing accumulated transactions at a regular daily, weekly, monthly, or quarterly schedule. Always secure a backup of your sales data so you can handle any unexpected situation. Sales records are important for preparing financial statement, making strategic plans, budgeting, and planning marketing strategies.

Inventory control is the recording of your materials, equipment, stocks, and other similar items on your business. Depending on your business, you can make monthly, quarterly or annual physical inventory. It is important that you keep every receipt of purchase on file with indication of equipment code number so you will not have any difficulty to do your inventory, evaluation and financial reports. There are various types of inventory control. The most current are:

- *Purchase order file* used to monitor purchase orders and their status;
- *Price book,* which maintains the record of purchase price, selling price, markdowns and markups, by supplier;
- *Want sheet,* recording items that are out-of-stock and that must be ordered.

## Staffing

Staffing your operations consists of assigning tasks to your employees. For business with chain of command, supervisors will assign tasks to immediate supervisees. The point is, an employee cannot come to work and guess what he/she is going to do or see the supervisor assigning him/her tasks to kill the time. This does not motivate at all, and may have serious uncovered consequences on the performance of your business. Also, take the time to observe and appreciate how productive your staff is and what the basis of their level of productivity is. You should also attempt to understand the strength of your employees, their level of commitment, and their career goals. This will help you make better use of your staff. Assign tasks to your employees based on their strength, and use cross training strategies so you can nurture a multi-task environment, which will be very beneficial for you business. Encourage team spirit and team activities as much as possible. Invite your employees to share their feedback with you. Do not penalize them for honest mistakes. Use their mistakes as opportunities for retraining and enhancement of personal commitment to the vision and mission of your business.

## Supervising

Some people do not need supervisory eyes to perform. Some others do. Then, every manager and supervisor in the chain of command must conduct random supervision to ensure that assigned tasks are being performed properly. I say random supervision, because you will not be able and do not have to control every move of your employees. This will affect negatively the performance of your business. Allow your employees some latitude to gossip sometime as long as this does not conflict with the completion deadline of an assignment.

Although your employees need supervision, you have to understand that they need their freedom to take risks and initiatives. This will be very helpful in making your business a reflecting and learning environment. Task delegation and accountability may be, in many cases effective supervisory strategies. You may want to rotate task delegation from time to time on the basis of fairness to reduce unnecessary conflicts and jealousy among employees.

Remember that an employee is an individual, a human being like you. Everyone has the right to be treated with respect and dignity. Make your employees feel that you treat them respectfully while you are supervising them. Communication is the key in that regard. Communication means primarily providing clear and non-equivocal instructions. Communication means that each employee is educated about the extent of his/her responsibility. Never assume that your supervisees need know something related to their tasks if you did not explain them. These are simple rules that can contribute to a healthy work environment.

# Motivating

Motivation is the drive that influences the actions of people. Motivation can be intrinsic or extrinsic. Intrinsic motivation refers to internal factors (want, desire, feeling, passion, etc) that make people act a certain way. On the other hand, extrinsic motivation is related to external factors (praise, reward, sanction, recognition, etc) that influence the action of individuals.

During the hiring process you can identify some aspects of the intrinsic motivation of potential employees. For example, you can ask them about their purpose in life, their expectation from a job, their priorities in life, their professional or career goals, and their hobbies. If the salary is the first motivation of an employee, chances are there is not too much of intrinsic motivation. While you have to pay your employees fairly, you would not make the right decision to hire someone who does not have a sense of purpose and an internal desire to have fun in the work place. Obviously, the work environment must encourage employees to have fun with the assignments, the clients, and with each other. A work environment that allows fun generates incredible energy, team spirit, positive attitudes, and enthusiasm. If the work environment is fun, the employee will be always excited to come to work. Sometimes, it is more appropriate to let employees spend some minutes to chat or share some jokes instead of pressing them to get things done with internal frustration.

You cannot create the intrinsic motivation of an employee, but you can secure it and help it grow through extrinsic motivation. As employer, you can influence the extrinsic motivation of your employees. The first step toward motivating your employees is creating a climate of empowerment, accountability and trust. You can empower your employees by educating them about the purpose of the business, give them more and more responsibilities and power to make emergency decisions and take calculated risks without fear of retaliation for unwelcomed outcomes. Empowerment gives employees ownership of their motivation and fosters greater accountability. Empowerment can help employees feel comfortable to let themselves be influenced by the vision and mission of your business. If you can create an environment of shared vision inside your company, you will have a team or group of cheerleaders who will do their best in terms of performance and productive.

Extrinsic motivation can also be influenced by acknowledging, recognizing, rewarding and celebrating the performance and achievement of your employees. Through the information system, you can set benchmarks and monitor performance and achievement that need to be recognized. Recognition alone is not enough. You have to set standardized criteria for rewarding employees that are recognized. The company must celebrate publicly with those employees that are recognized for their achievements or performance. Celebrations for recognition and reward should take place on a quarterly basis. Recognition and reward files must be taken into consideration during annual performance appraisal.

## Evaluating

In the planning forms, you have indicators of measurement that can help you evaluate whether you achieved your objectives or not. Evaluation in operations management is very important to help monitor progress, correct mistakes, and make adjustments or changes. Here is an evaluation form that you may find useful:

**Figure 19**
**Evaluation form**

Business name
Evaluation Form

Prepared by: _____ Position:_____

Period From_____ To _____

| Planned activity | Accomplished activity | Date | Indicator | Reflecting/ Learning challenges |
|---|---|---|---|---|
| | | | | |
| | | | | |
| | | | | |
| | | | | |
| | | | | |

## DO IT YOURSELF!

1. Make a weekly plan of activities for your staff.

2. Explain in a few paragraphs what a day of business will look like for your company!

3. Indicate a list of strategies and techniques that you think you can use effectively to motivate your employees toward greater productivity!

# Chapter VI
## Personnel Management

An entrepreneur does not have to hire staff when first starting a business. There is nothing wrong with that if this is your jump start strategy. In fact, many small business entrepreneurs succeed at doing that. Other small business owners will have to hire in the beginning. Even those who started without hiring will have to deal with the hiring issue sooner or later if they really mean business. Then, by any means, hiring is a must in doing business, whether it is about independent contractors, part-time or full-time employees.

To a large extent, effective management depends on effective hiring, because, knowledge and commitment of the best people are the main factors that make a company prosper. While a company workforce is priceless, its hiring is a critical decision that must be made with effectiveness and prudence. It is not useful at all to have a workforce that is going to turn over because of bad hires. Hiring is very costly. Turn over is costly as well. In fact, if a company has a high employee turn over rate, there is a management or leadership problem that should be investigated somewhere in this company.

## Hiring: the ARSH approach

You may want to use the ARSH approach that I suggest when you are hiring. The ARSH approach is an acronym in which the four letters stand respectively for assessing (A), reaching (R), screening (S), and hiring (H).

## *Assessing*

Assessing is the process of identifying and expressing in writing your hiring needs. If you do not know who you are looking for and what you will precisely ask him/her to do, it will be very difficult for you to hire the right people for your business. It may sound redundant, but it is not. The assessing process includes determining the profile of the employee that you are seeking, the job description, and compensation, and benefits.

- *Employee profile*: To determine the employee profile, you need to be able to answer questions such as: Do I need an employee that has the potentiality to share the vision and mission of my business, whatever his/her function is? Do I need an employee that is just looking for a pay check? Do I need an employee that has strengths that can contribute to the growth of my business? Do I need an employee that has strengths not closely related to my business, but I can build on to make my business prosper? Do I need an employee with multitask potentiality? Do I need someone flexible, reliable, with a sense of respect, honesty, dignity, responsibility, and a positive spirit? You may raise other similar questions of your choice. You need to put the profile of the employee that you are looking for in writing, and seek for this profile during the screening process.
- *Job description*: The job description details the job position title, the supervisory relationships, a job summary, the specifics about duties and responsibilities, the approximate percentage of work time allocation per duty, the salary range, and the qualifications of the person for such position.

Here is a sample of a job description format:

## Figure 20
## Format of a job description

| Business Name<br>Job Title:<br>Supervisor:<br>Number of subordinates:<br>Salary range: | | |
|---|---|---|
| Qualifications | | |
| Job Summary | | |
| Duty # | Description | Approximate percentage of work time allocation per duty |
| 1 | | x% |
| 2 | | x% |
| 3 | | x% |
| 4 | | x% |
| 5 | | x% |
| 6 | | x% |

Here is an example of job description:

**Figure 21**
**Sample of Job Description**

**Job Description**

**Job Title**: Accountant
**Supervisor**: Chief Financial Officer
**Number of subordinates**: 0
**Salary range**: Based on experience and qualifications.

## Qualifications

Associate degree in finance or business administration in combination with financial management experience. Bachelor degree preferred. Committed, tough minded, pragmatic, performance-driven personality. Must be proficient in a Windows environment, including word processing, outlook, and power point, spreadsheet, and database software. Ability to work within a team setting with multiple contributors on projects. Ability to multi-task projects, people and events to get the job done. Willingness to learn new things and eagerness to acquire new skills. Valid Florida driver's license. Two references required.

## Job Summary

Under the direction of the Chief Executive Officer (CEO) the Chief Financial Officer (CFO) is responsible for adding value to the company through the acquisition and management of financial and information technology resources. As a member of the senior management team, the CFO directs, plans, controls and coordinates the overall financial activities of the organization, and will directly manage the ABC Finance, Treasury and Cash Management, Tax and Regulatory Compliance, Accounting & Reporting, Information Systems, Planning, Forecasting, Budgeting, Credit and Collection, as well as office and facilities management. The CFO will establish and maintain relationships with lending institutions and the financial community. The CFO will be responsible for directing the financial strategy of the organization ensuring that adequate financial resources will be available to accomplish its mission, a the same time, managing the costs of acquiring these resources. The CFO directs the Planning efforts through coordination with Operational Managers to develop the Long-Range Plan and the Annual Operating Plan. Analyses business aspects beyond compilation of numbers. Provides planning and analytical expertise. Along with the other members of senior management, the CFO accurately and completely represents the Company to funders, lenders and the financial community. This activity can result in significant value added by reducing the cost of capital. Develops creative means of financing business acquisitions and other capital expenditures and initiatives. The CFO manages cash flow, investments and credit lines to maximize productivity of the Company's financial resources. The CFO directs the Accounting function in providing the necessary systems, internal controls and reports such that the Company's assets are safeguarded, costs controlled, and assets deployed in the most efficient manner.

| Duty # | Description | Approximate percentage of work time allocation per duty |
|---|---|---|
| 1 | Prepares monthly, quarterly, and annual financial statements in accordance with GAAP. Preparing periodic reports of budgets and forecasts for management, with particular attention to cash flow, forecasts and revenue projections. | 5 % |
| 2 | Responsible for developing short and long term financial plans and forecasts as well as overseeing a senior accountant and related staff. | 10% |

| 3 | Performs cost accounting and ratio analysis of various aspects and units of the organization as needed, with an eye on improving profitability. | 10% |
|---|---|---|
| 4 | Directs the Information Systems function to ensure that appropriate, accurate and timely information is supplied to operational management. | 10% |
| 5 | Develops monitors and implements necessary changes in the organization's system of internal controls such that the organization's assets are safeguarded and information is reported accurately and in a timely manner. | 10% |
| 6 | Oversees preparation and filing of all federal, state and local income tax returns for the organization. | 5 % |
| 7 | Oversees preparation and filing of all pension forms and related documentation; Ensures compliance with all outside regulatory agencies and organizations; Coordinates with other department heads to assist with compliance issues as they arise. Works closely with external Auditors. | 10% |
| 8 | Acts as primary contact with banking and lending community Responsible for developing and instituting long and short term borrowing plans with outside sources; Institutes cash management policies to maximize short term yield; Responsible for the establishment of formal credit policies; Oversees collections of accounts receivable to ensure minimum aging of accounts. | 10% |
| 9 | Directs the inventory accounting function. Provides information and analysis on a timely basis to operating groups to identify opportunities and risks. | 10% |

| 10 | Works with senior management to develop strategies for maintaining profitable growth; Develops methodologies for enhancing and documenting all policies and procedures; Participates in the identification and due diligence of possible partnerships; Oversees the implementation of standard operating procedures and cutting edge technologies throughout the organization. Performs related duties as assigned. | 20% |
|---|---|---|

**CONDITIONS OF EMPLOYMENT**

This position is subject to the terms and conditions specified in the employment contract. Work is normally performed in a typical interior/office work environment. No or very limited physical effort required. No or very limited exposure to physical risk. The ABC provides all training required by OSHA to ensure employee safety.

- *Compensation and benefits*: People work primarily to get paid and for many other reasons. In other words, when you consider hiring employees, you have to think about their compensation. I would advise to have a salary grid for your business based on criteria such as level of education, length of experience, and special working conditions (whether it is a second or third shift hours, for example). You can determine your base salary range by comparing with other businesses similar to yours. There are many sources such as the U.S Department of Labor's Bureau of Labor Statistics, the Chamber of Commerce of your area, or other consulting or professional corporations. Make an effort to pay your employees something more than other similar competitor businesses do. You will get it back through stronger commitment of the employees to your business. For example, you may earn hundreds, thousands of dollars of benefits from one dollar or two dollars increase that you give to employees with outstanding performance when such employees expected this raise the least. If your employees are underpaid, the performance and prosperity of your business will pay the price daily.

In addition to compensation, there are some employee benefits that you may consider:

- Life insurance,
- Retirement plan,
- Medical care,
- Paid holidays,
- Paid vacations,
- Paid jury duty leave,
- Paid sick leave,
- Paid maternity leave,
- Paid funeral leave.

*Reaching*

The reaching process involves how your potential employees reach you or how you reach them. There are several ways such as help-wanted advertising, job fair, internal referrals, newspaper, internet/world wide web, employment agencies, and other similar means.

*Screening*

Screening a potential employee is where many managers make the mistake that costs a lot of money and even reputation to their business or company. This is the phase where you conduct the interviews, obtain the background check, obtain a second opinion, and check references, before you decide whether to hire someone.

*Interview:* Before spending the time to conduct an interview, make sure that you reviewed the application or the resume, and you had a preliminary phone contact, if possible. Before you conduct the interview, write down your questions on paper, and let the interviewee be aware that you are taking note of what he/she is saying. Your questions should be based on the profile that you defined for your hiring needs. Be aware of discriminatory questions or comments related to age, marital status, national origin, race, sexual orientation, handicap, and religion and political beliefs. For some positions in your business you may have to conduct more than one interview.

*Second opinion*: It is always good to have a second opinion on a candidate that you feel like hiring.

*Background check*: If the position requires a background check, do not neglect to obtain it before you make any hiring decision.

*Checking references*: Always check the references that a candidate gave you. Call or send a fill out – return form to the address provided.

*Hiring*

By hiring I mean the orientation process, the job offer letter and the signing of an employment contract. Before you hire someone, consider doing an orientation first to observe your new "employee". Issue a job offer letter. Usually, a job offer letter is written in the business letterhead, and includes:
- The date of the letter,
- The name and address of the person,
- A salutation or/and congratulation paragraph,
- A sentence making a formal offer of employment,
- The job position,
- The compensation and eventual benefits (including when? and how?)
- The date of the first salary review,
- The orientation period that will follow this offer,
- The signing of a contract.

## Personnel Policies and Procedures

It is almost a cliché to say that the personnel are the greatest asset of a small business. You understand that your business cannot grow without the proper performance of your employees. You may start your business without employees, but it cannot grow without them. Consequently, there must be policies in place, so your relationships with the personnel will not hurt the business. The personnel policies must be in place before employees come in. When you have employees, you may adjust the policies, so they can be responsive to their needs. The following paragraphs will present an example of personnel policies and procedures that you may want to adapt for your small business.

*Introductory Statement*

Usually, a personnel policies document starts with an introductory statement, which indicates the objectives, or goals that such a document aims to achieve, the information included, and the target readers, obviously the employees of the business. Here is an example of "introductory statement":

> *This personnel policies and procedures handbook applies to all employees, and is intended to provide guidelines and summary information about ABC Computer's personnel policies, procedures, benefits, and rules of conduct.*
>
> *It is important that you read, understand, and become familiar with the handbook and comply with the standards that have been established. Please contact your supervisor if you have any questions or need additional information.*
>
> *Obviously, this handbook does not anticipate every situation that may arise in the workplace or provide information that answers every possible question. As a result, ABC Computer, Inc. reserves the right to modify, supplement or revise any policy, benefit, or provision from time to time, with or without notice, when it is necessary. The information in this employee handbook supersedes and replaces all previous personnel policies, procedures, benefits, and rules of conduct. For the purpose of this handbook, "employee" and "staff member" will be considered one in the same.*

*Employment and the legislation*

The definition and legal implications of employment must be clarified in such a way that you and your employees have the same understanding of that relationship. If you and your employees do not agree on what employment in your small business is as well as what the legal implications are, you risk generating unnecessary conflicts. While a small business enjoys the benefits of employment at-will agreement, a small business owner must be aware of the employment legislations. The personnel policies must be reflective of them. For example,

- The Civil Rights Act, 1964, declares all discriminatory employment practices unlawful;
- The Equal Employment Opportunity Act, 1972, extends the benefits of the Civil Rights Act to all kinds of businesses;
- The Rehabilitation Act, 1973, and the Americans with Disabilities Act, 1990, prohibits discrimination against persons with disabilities;
- The Age Discrimination in Employment Act, 1967, protects persons age 40 and older against discriminatory employment practices.

These are a few among a repertoire of employment legislations that you must be aware of when hiring and dealing with your employees. The following paragraphs give an example of the insertion of the employment legislations in the personnel policies:

> *Employment at will agreement: Employment is with the mutual consent of you and ABC Computer. Consequently, both you and ABC Computer have the right to terminate the employment relationship at any time, with or without cause or advance notice. This employment at will agreement constitutes the entire agreement between you and ABC Computer on the subject of termination and it supersedes all prior agreements. Although other policies and procedures of ABC Computer may change from time to time, this employment at will agreement will remain in effect throughout your employment with ABC Computer unless it is specifically modified by an express written agreement signed by you and the General Manager of ABC Computer. This employment at will agreement may not be modified by any oral or implied agreement.*

> *Equal employment opportunity: ABC Computer is committed to equal employment opportunity for all qualified persons,*

*regardless of race, color, gender, national origin, or sexual orientation. This applies to all employment practices. All employees must show respect and sensitivity toward all other employees, and demonstrate a commitment to ABC Computer's equal opportunity goals. If you observe a violation of this policy, you are expected to report it immediately to your supervisor or the Personnel Team. ABC Computer will promptly investigate any complaint and take appropriate preventative and/or corrective action. Violation of this policy may result in disciplinary action, up to and including possible termination.*

*Immigration reform and control act of 1986: ABC Computer is committed to full compliance with the federal immigration laws and will not knowingly hire or continue to employ anyone who does not have the legal right to work in the United States. As an ongoing condition of employment, you will be required to provide documentation verifying your identity and legal authority to work in the United States.*

*Employee classifications: ABC Computer classifies employees in the following ways:*

*Full Time Salaried Employee - you are considered to be a full time employee if your budgeted average hours of work each workweek are more than 32 hours.*

*Part Time Hourly Employee - you are considered to be a part time employee if your budgeted average hours of work each workweek are 32 hours or less.*

*Employment of relatives: Relatives of employees will receive the same consideration as any other applicant for a job opening. They will not be accorded preferential treatment in employment matters. However, related employees may not be permitted to work in the same department or under the direct supervision of each other because of employee morale, security, or other legitimate business reasons. In addition,*

*ABC Computer may require a related employee to transfer or resign if there is a conflict of interest or management problem of supervision that cannot be resolved.*

*Benefits*

You will not be able to retain good employees if you do not provide satisfactory benefits. The benefits provided must be clearly explained in the policies manual. This helps the employees not only have a tangible meaning of what the benefits are, but also an awareness of the proper procedures to utilize them. Vacation, holidays, sick days, leave of absence, health insurance coverage, educational assistance, and workers' compensation are some of the items that must be clarified and explained to employees. The following paragraphs will illustrate what the wording will look like:

*Vacation: Employees will earn vacation time based on the following schedule:*

> *1 week paid after 1 year of employment*
> *2 weeks paid after 2 years of employment*
> *3 weeks paid after 3 years of employment*
> *4 weeks paid after 10 years of employment*

*Part time employees are eligible for the same benefits based on the percentage of time spent in their work; e.g. a person who works 2 days per week (40% of full time) would be eligible for 2 days vacation per year after the first year and 4 days after the second year. A day of vacation benefit is equal to the length of the day the employee works.*

*One week of vacation time may be carried over into the next year. Employees who are leaving employment will be allowed to take earned vacation hours before the last day of employment or be paid for earned vacation hours.*

*Holiday pay: Employees will be eligible to receive holiday pay on the following holidays:*

*New Years Day*
*Christmas Day*
*Labor Day*
*Memorial Day*
*Thanksgiving Day*
*Independence Day*

> *The rate of pay will be 20% of the budgeted weekly pay of the employee.*

*The following general provisions apply to holiday pay:*

> *Only holidays which fall on a week day will be paid.*
> *If a holiday falls during an employee's approved vacation period, the employee will receive holiday pay, and will not be charged for a vacation day on the day the holiday is observed. Employees on leave of absence for any reason are not eligible for holiday pay on holidays that are observed while they are on leave.*
> *Holiday pay will not count as hours worked for the calculation of overtime.*

> *Sick days: Employees will be eligible to earn up to 3 days of sick pay for each year of full time employment. Sick pay benefits may be accumulated up to a maximum of ten days. Employees who accumulate the maximum benefit allowed will not earn additional sick pay benefits until their accumulated total has been reduced below the maximum.*

> *Sick pay benefits will only be earned up to the maximum amount.*

> *The Personnel Team will review unusual circumstances requiring more than 2 weeks of sick leave when such circumstances arise on an individual basis. Such recommendations will be forwarded to the General manager for final determination.*

*Leaves of absence:*

> *Family and Medical Leave: Eligible staff members will be entitled to a total of 12 work weeks of unpaid leave during any moving 12 month period after the first qualifying date for one or more of the following:*

1. *Because of the birth of a son or daughter of the staff member, and in order to care for such son or daughter.*
2. *Because of the placement of a son or daughter with the staff member for adoption or foster care.*
3. *In order to care for an immediate family member if such immediate family member has a serious health condition; and*
4. *Because of a serious health condition that makes the staff member unable to perform the functions of the position of such staff member.*

> *Personal leave: An unpaid leave of absence not covered by the Family and Medical Leave Policy may be granted in the case of a personal emergency. Each leave will be evaluated on its own merit by the Personnel Team of ABC Computer.*

*Bereavement Leave: In the event of the death of a member of a staff member's family, the following bereavement pay will be allowed:*

| | |
|---|---|
| *Husband or wife* | *One week* |
| *Son or daughter* | *One week* |
| *Mother or father* | *Three days* |
| *Brother or sister* | *Three days* |
| *Grandparent* | *Three days* |
| *Grandchild* | *Three days* |
| *Mother-in-law or father-in-law* | *Three days* |
| *Brother-in-law or sister-in-law* | *Three days* |

> *These benefits would apply to step relationships as well. Other circumstances are at the discretion of the supervisor and the Personnel Team of ABC Computer.*

> *Jury or Witness Duty: Any staff member called to jury duty*

*or called as a witness will be compensated for normal hours/ salary at the normal pay rate, less the amount compensated by the court.*

*Study Leave: A leave of absence for personal growth and professional advancement for management staff is subject to the original terms of employment.*

*Military Leave: Leave of absence is available to those staff members who enter military service.*

*Workers' Compensation Leave: ABC Computer complies with applicable state and federal law concerning leaves for work-related illness or injury.*

*The following general provisions apply to all leaves of absence: A request for an extension of a leave of absence must be made in writing prior to the expiration date of the original leave, and when appropriate, must be accompanied by a physician's written statement that certifies the need for the extension.*

*Failure to return to work on the first workday following the expiration of an approved leave of absence may be considered a voluntary termination.*

*Health insurance coverage: Health insurance coverage is available for all employees and their families, subject to the terms of their employment.*

*Workers' compensation insurance: All employees are automatically covered by Workers' Compensation Insurance at the time they are hired. ABC Computer pays 100% of the premiums for this important coverage. The following benefits are provided to employees who sustain a work-related injury or illness:*
- *partial wage replacement for periods of disability;*
- *medical care, including medicine, hospital, doctor, X-rays, crutches, etc.;*
- *rehabilitation services, if necessary.*

*It is important that you report any work-related injury or illness to your supervisor, as soon as it happens, regardless of how minor it may be. It is also important to get proper first aid and/or medical attention immediately.*

*Educational assistance and professional memberships: Where it can be demonstrated that ABC Computer will benefit from an employee's participation in an educational program or professional organization, the related expenses may be paid by ABC Computer. Requests for payment of expenses related to educational programs and professional organizations must be approved in advance by the Personnel Team of ABC Computer.*

*Personnel Status*

Personnel status includes policies regarding the records of employees, tardiness and absence, promotion, demotion, transfer, and termination. When hired by your business, an employee must know what will happen in case of repetitive absences and tardiness. The employee must also know what factors are related to promotion, demotion, transfer, or termination. These items of the personnel policies will seriously affect the productivity and performance of your employees. The policies must make explicit this fact. However, keep in mind that employees are human beings. There may be unforeseen situations that can explain tardiness or absence. The policies must exist, but do not abuse them. Try to find additional tools so you can inspire intrinsic motivation to the employees. For example, the employee must be aware that if he/she comes late, it is an obligation to work for extra minutes or hours. Create a culture of personnel accountability that is linked with the policies in place. This will make the policies the last resort when making disciplinary decisions. Here is how the policies regarding personnel status might be formulated:

*Personnel records: It is important that ABC Computer maintain current information about you. Please let the*

*Financial Coordinator know immediately if you change your name, address, phone number, or marital status, etc.*

*At reasonable times and on reasonable notice, you will be allowed to review any personnel records that have been used to determine your qualifications for employment, promotion, compensation, termination, or other disciplinary action.*

*Tardiness and absence: Employees must work their assigned schedules as consistently as possible. However, ABC Computer understands that because of illness or emergency you may be unable to come to work.*

*If you are unable to report to work for any reason, you must notify your immediate supervisor. It is your responsibility to keep ABC Computer informed on a daily basis during a short-term absence and to provide medical verification when asked to do so.*

*Employees who do not call in or report to work on time may be subject to disciplinary action, up to and including termination.*

*Time cards: Staff members who are paid on an hourly basis, must prepare time cards for each week that they should be paid. Staff members should record daily the time they arrive at and leave work. In the event the staff member is on vacation or is entitled to holiday pay, a time card must be submitted. Nonexempt hourly employees will not be paid for more than the budgeted average weekly amount without prior approval. Time cards are due every Friday by 2:00 p.m. to the Financial Coordinator. Completed time cards must be signed by the staff member and supervisor. Failure to turn time cards in on time or turning in cards not signed by proper personnel may result in delay of payment.*

*Promotion, demotion, and transfer: It is the intent of ABC Computer to give qualified employees preference over others when filling job openings within the company. However, because of the experience, skills, and educational requirements of many jobs, promotions from within ABC Computer are not always possible. An employee's past performance, experience, attitude, qualifications, and potential are all important factors which will be considered in making promotion and transfer decisions. ABC Computer reserves the right to promote, transfer and demote employees, at its sole discretion, with or without cause or advance notice.*

*Disciplinary and exiting procedures: ABC Computer is an "at will" employer. ABC Computer or the staff member may terminate employment "at will" with or without notice, with or without cause.*

*Disciplinary procedures: Whenever it is determined that a staff member has committed a disciplinary offense, the staff member's supervisor and the Personnel Team will decide upon an appropriate disciplinary action. The range of disciplinary action may include written warning, suspension, or discharge. The appropriateness of the penalty in each case will be determined by the Personnel Team depending on its judgment as to the seriousness of the offense, the staff member's prior history and other relevant circumstances.*

*Written warning: A record of the meeting stating the facts and the action taken will be prepared by the supervisor. The supervisor will then review the warning memo with the staff member, and ask the staff member to sign it. One copy will go to the Personnel Team and another copy will be placed in the staff member's personnel file.*

*Termination of Employment: It is the policy of ABC Computer to make every effort to avoid unwarranted discharges. However, it is necessary to enforce our policies fairly and consistently. Violations of the policies will result in one or more of the disciplinary actions according to the frequency, seriousness and circumstances of the offense. ABC*

*Computer believes that termination is the last choice and that other alternatives should be pursued diligently before termination would happen.*

Termination:

*Voluntary termination: Termination that is initiated by the employee. We request two weeks written notice from you before you leave your job. Please advise your supervisor of your last day of work.*

*Involuntary termination: Termination that is initiated by ABC Computer for reasons other than changing budgetary conditions.*

*Layoff: Termination of employment that results from changing budgetary conditions which necessitate a reduction in staff. Whenever ABC Computer determines, in its sole discretion, a layoff should occur, the following factors will be among those considered: versatility, qualifications, skill, ability, performance, efficiency, loyalty, attitude, and dependability.*

*Exit procedures - All employees will be required to process through the supervisor and/or Personnel Team before receiving final pay. This process will include an exit interview, turning in keys, cell phones, email pass codes, and any other ABC Computer property.*

Compensation

The personnel policies also provide information about payday, wages and salary reviews, and payroll deductions. The formulation of compensation policies in the manual might be as follows:

*Pay period: A pay period is a two week period of time that begins on Monday and ends on Sunday. Employees are generally paid on the Monday one day after the end of each pay period.*

*Wage and salary reviews: Employees are generally reviewed once a year for consideration of a wage or salary increase. An annual review does not imply an automatic wage or salary increase.*

*Payroll deductions: You are probably familiar with the various payroll deductions that are required by law, such as federal income tax, state income tax, state disability insurance, Medicare and social security taxes. Any other deductions from your paycheck must be authorized by you, in writing. ABC Computer complies with applicable state and federal laws regarding the garnishment and assignment of wages.*

*Other payroll deduction options include:*

*401(k) Plan – This is a tax deferred retirement plan available to employees of ABC Computer. Employees are allowed to designate a dollar amount to be deducted from each paycheck to be placed in their 401(k) account. This deduction is prior to Federal and State tax deductions. This deduction is purely at the employee's discretion and is not matched by ABC Computer contributions. For further information, contact the Financial Coordinator.*

*Each one of your paycheck stubs will itemize amounts that have been withheld. It is important that you keep this information for tax purposes. If you have any questions about your deductions, please contact the Financial Coordinator.*

*Performance and Staff Relations*

Your small business must provide employees incentive to work at their best. A performance evaluation system is an appropriate tool that can be used to appraise performance based on job description and performance standards. A fair performance management system will positively affect staff relations. The section of personnel policies regarding performance and staff relations might be written as follows:

*Job descriptions: Employees are given a job description before they start to work. A job description summarizes your duties and responsibilities and gives you important information about your new job. Please read and study your job description carefully and discuss it with your supervisor if you have any questions. ABC Computer reserves the right to revise and update your job description from time to time, as it deems necessary and appropriate.*

*Performance evaluations: Employees will receive a written performance evaluation after approximately six months of service, and annually thereafter. The purpose of the performance evaluation is to discuss your performance and to identify expectations and goals for the future. Written performance evaluations may include commendation for good work, as well as specific recommendations for improvement.*

*You will have the opportunity to discuss your performance evaluation with your supervisor. This is a good time to ask questions and clarify important points. Performance evaluations help ABC Computer make important decisions about job placement, training and development.*

*Problem solving procedures: The following guidelines are established to help staff members voice their opinions and discuss their problems and concerns.*
*The first discussion and attempted resolution should generally be through the supervisor first.*
*If the situation is not resolved satisfactorily, then an appointment should be scheduled with the next supervisors in the chain of command.*
*If the issue is still not resolved, the staff member may request to meet with the General Manager. This request should be made through the General Manager.*

*General Information*

Depending on the need of the company the personnel policies and procedures manual may provide additional information to better manage employment relations. For example, this section can include policies regarding sexual harassment, use of drugs and alcohol, use of business materials and equipment, use of the internet, dressing codes, and all other items that can contribute to a better human resource management of a business. The following are some examples of general policy information:

> *Policy against harassment: ABC Computer is committed to providing a work environment that is free of discrimination. In keeping with this commitment, ABC Computer maintains a strict policy prohibiting unlawful harassment, including sexual harassment.*

> *Sexual harassment of employees by supervisors, co-workers, or vendors is prohibited. Unlawful sexual harassment includes unwelcome sexual advances, requests for sexual favors, and other verbal, visual, or physical conduct of a sexual nature when:*
> *-submission to the conduct is made a condition of employment;*
> *-submission to or rejection of the conduct is used as the basis for an employment decision affecting the harassed employee; or*
> *-the harassment has the purpose or effect of unreasonably interfering with an employee's work performance or creates an intimidating, hostile, or offensive work environment.*

> *If you believe that you are being, or have been, harassed in any way, you are expected to report the facts of the incident or incidents to your supervisor or the Personnel Team immediately, without fear of reprisal. In determining whether the alleged conduct constitutes unlawful harassment, the totality of the circumstances, such as the nature of the conduct and the context in which the alleged incident occurred, will be investigated.*

*Violation of this policy may result in disciplinary action, up to and including termination.*

*It is prohibited to use, sell, transfer, possess, or be "under the influence" of alcohol, drugs, or controlled substances when on duty, on ABC Computer property, or in ABC Computer vehicle.*

*Violation of this policy may result in disciplinary action, up to and including termination.*

*All employees are prohibited from engaging in outside employment, private business, or other activity, which might have an adverse effect on, or create a conflict of interest with ABC Computer.*

*Your appearance reflects not only on you as an individual, but on ABC Computer as well. We expect you to take pride in your appearance and strive to achieve a positive image when representing ABC Computer.*

*ABC Computer will not be responsible for personal property that is lost, damaged, stolen, or destroyed. If you happen to find personal belongings that have been lost by another person, please turn them in to your supervisor.*

*It is important that ABC Computer have access at all times to company property, as well as other records, documents, and files. As a result, ABC Computer reserves the right to access employee offices, work stations, filing cabinets, desks, computers, computer files, voice mail, e-mail, and any other company property at its discretion, with or without advance notice or consent.*

*Employees will be reimbursed for all approved company-related expenses, upon submission of accurate and receipted expense reports to ABC Computer. Employees are requested to submit these reports in a timely manner to ensure proper accounting and prompt reimbursement.*

*Employees are expected to use good judgment and common sense when it comes to personal communication. Employees who violate this policy may be subject to disciplinary action, up to and including termination.*

*Staff members may use their computers for personal use when not working. Any and all devices from an outside source must be checked for a virus before using it on any company computer.*

*Staff members accessing the Internet are representing ABC Computer. All communications should be for professional reasons. Staff members are responsible for seeing that the Internet is used in an effective, ethical and lawful manner.*

*The Internet should not be used for personal gain or advancement of individual views. Solicitation of non-company business, or any use of the Internet for personal gain, is strictly prohibited.*

*To prevent computer viruses from being transmitted through the system, there will be no unauthorized downloading of any software. All software downloading must first be authorized through the General Manager of ABC Computer.*

*Copyrighted materials belonging to entities other than ABC Computer may not be transmitted by staff members on the Internet. One copy of copyrighted material may be downloaded for your own personal research. Users are not permitted to copy, transfer, rename, add or delete information or programs belonging to other users unless given written permission to do so by the owner. Failure to observe copyright or license agreements may result in disciplinary action from ABC Computer or legal action by the copyright owner.*

*Harassment of any kind is prohibited. No messages with derogatory or inflammatory remarks about an individual or group's race, religion, national origin, physical attributes, or sexual orientation may be transmitted.*

## Conclusion

The examples given in this chapter can be adapted based on the needs of your small business to write your own personnel policies. Some of them are the general wording used in the personnel policies manual of most companies. There is a tendency to say "I am not hiring right now, I don't need a personnel policy." This is not a good idea, unless you don't really mean business. The policies must be in place before you start hiring. If you open your business and things start working unexpectedly well, you will need to hire people. What will happen if you don't have policies in place to manage your relationships with your employee(s)? You may tend to cultivate a verbal relationship, which can be unlawful in so many areas. This is a risk that is not worth taking. Your policies may not be perfect in the beginning. This is not a problem. It can be improved. The problem is to not have policies in place.

## DO IT YOURSELF!

1. Write a job description to hire a manager for your business.

2. Write a job posting to hire a manager for your business. Include information on qualifications and job summary about the position.

3. Write in one or two paragraphs the profile of your ideal employee.

4. You are organizing an orientation session for a new employee. Make

- A list of documents that you will need for this session.
- An outline of key information that you think you must communicate to the new employee.

# CHAPTER VII
## Financial management

Financial management is a set of strategies and practices that help you manage the revenues that your business generates and control your expenses. Effective financial management can help maximize your profits and minimize the costs. In matters of financial management you will have to handle issues of budgeting, bookkeeping and banking, income statement, cash flow, balance sheet, purchase, credit, and taxes.

Effective financial management practices requires that you have accounting policies and procedures in place, in order to ensure that assets are safeguarded, financial statement are in compliance with Generally Accepted Accounting Principles (GAAP), and finances are managed with appropriate and effective stewardship. A manual or a written document must be generated to avoid miscommunication and administrative catastrophe.

## Financial Accountability

The people in charge of making financial decisions and endorsing financial accountability must be determined and the information must be communicated to all employees. Let's assume, for example, you have a general manager, and administrative manager, a financial coordinator, and an office assistant, to endorse financial accountability. The responsibilities could be defined as follows:

*General Manager:*
- Reviews and approves all financial reports.
- Reviews and approves annual budget.
- Reviews the payroll summary for the correct payee, hours worked and check amount.
- Reviews all vouchers and invoices for those checks which require his or her signature.
- Check signing authority on all company accounts.
- Authorizes expenditures in excess of $10,000, except preapproved capital expenditures (such as rent) which might exceed $10,000.
- Reviews and approves all contracts for goods and services that will exceed $10,000 over the year.

*Administrative Manager:*
- Approves all vouchers, invoices and checks.
- Receives unopened bank statements.
- With the Financial Coordinator, and input from the General Manager and Team leaders, develops the annual budget.
- Reviews and approves all financial reports.
- Reviews and approves list of pending check disbursements.
- Reviews all vouchers and invoices for those checks which require his or her signature.
- Authorizes all inter-fund transfers.
- Reviews all bank reconciliations.
- Reviews the payroll summary for the correct payee, hours worked and check amount.
- Approves all reimbursements.
- Manages the assets accounts.

*Financial Coordinator:*
- Processes all receipts and disbursements.
- Processes the payroll, including payroll tax returns.
- Submits requests for inter-fund transfers.
- Maintains and reconciles the general ledger monthly.
- With the Administrative Manager, and with input from the

General Manager and Team leaders, develops the annual budget.
- Prepares all financial reports, including requests for reimbursements.
- Manages the petty cash fund.
- Reconciles the bank accounts.
- Reconciles the statement of credit card deposits and service charges.
- Double checks all reimbursement requests against receipts provided.

*Office Assistant*:
- Receives and opens all incoming mail, except the bank statements.
- Prepares cash receipts log and invoice log.
- Prepares all checks for payments.
- Processes credit card payments for publications.

## Cash Handling

Usually, the Office Assistant should receive all incoming mail, including cash. All checks received by the Office Assistant should be recorded on a cash receipts log which states the unit to which the income is attributed, and stamped "**for deposit only**". Following reception, the Office Assistant would then make two copies of the check with one copy forwarded to the financial coordinator and the other copy to the transaction file. A copy of the cash receipts log should be given to the administrative manager on a daily basis or according to the appropriate schedule.

It should be the responsibility of the financial coordinator to prepare a deposit slip and deposit the funds into the savings account of the company. The financial coordinator should record all deposit and cash receipts in the appropriate log and according to month received. The financial coordinator should ensure that any deposit not forwarded or mailed to the bank be locked in the appropriate lock box for up to 24 hours. If the funds are mailed to the bank, the financial coordinator should indicate the date mailed and received on the cash receipts log.

The financial coordinator should make a copy of each check mailed and file them in a separate file folder. Finally, the financial coordinator should remember that the FDIC will not ensure an amount of more than $ 250,000. Therefore, no single account should contain more than the amount over which the FDIC will not insure.

Request for wire transfer should be prepared by the financial coordinator and should be signed by the administrative or the general manager. The financial coordinator should monitor the transfer of funds and maintain the appropriate records of such transaction. As soon as the funds are credited to the company savings account, the bank usually sends a credit memo to the financial coordinator or the equivalent person. The financial coordinator should reconcile these credit memos to the total cash received at the end of the month.

It is considered good practice for small business to avoid operating a checking account that exceeds $10,000 at any time. All funds received should be deposited into the savings account. Funds can be transferred from the savings account into the checking account when needed.

The financial coordinator should monitor the balance in the checking account, and determine if there are adequate funds to pay the daily expenses. The financial coordinator should prepare a transfer memo for signature by the administrative manager to transfer the necessary amounts from the savings account to the checking account, as long as the remaining balance does not exceed $10,000. These transfers may occur concurrently with the associated disbursements.

A company can allow the Office Assistant to be responsible for processing the receipt of funds through the credit card authorizer directly into the savings account. These transactions can be processed on a weekly basis, with a list of the credits and date processed, delivered to the financial coordinator in order to double check against the bank statements. However, the reconciliation of the statement of deposits and service charges remain the responsibility of the financial coordinator.

Incoming invoices received should be logged in by the Office Assistant (naming the staff person responsible for ordering the product or service) and delivered to the appropriate staff person for approval and to prepare a check request voucher prior to disbursement dates.

The staff person responsible for ordering the product or service should check the validity of an invoice against proposals/bids, and work accomplished/delivered and prepares a check request voucher prior to disbursement dates.

The financial coordinator should be responsible to prepare cash disbursement for signature by authorized officials in matters related to expenses, debts, and liabilities. This could be done twice monthly. For effective recording, all disbursements should be made by check unless the item is considered a petty cash item.

A check request voucher should be completed by the purchasing staff person and attached to the original vendor invoice, and/or any other supporting documentation. The voucher should include the account codes to which the expense will be applied. Approval for an expense by the authorized staff must be indicated on the check request voucher.

The financial coordinator should prepare a master list of all checks to be paid for approval by the general manager or administrative manager. If there are any questions or concerns about the amounts, the financial coordinator should provide necessary information prior to running any disbursements. If there are any items removed from the batch, the totals on the payment summary form should be corrected, initialed and dated by the general manager or administrative manager.

The financial coordinator should then run an aging account payable. A total of the disbursements to be paid could be recorded on the form and sent to the administrative manager for approval, along with the current balance in any and all cash accounts. Upon reception of the amount to be disbursed, the financial coordinator can print the checks and attach them to the invoice, and other supporting documentation, being paid and submitted for signatures.

The financial coordinator should double check the check request voucher to ensure the account is charged to the correct expense and line item. After the checks have been signed, the second signatory should double check the work, cancel the invoice by stamping "PAID" on it in red ink, and pass the checks on to the Office Assistant for mailing.

At least, once monthly, the financial coordinator should check the invoice log to determine if there are any outstanding invoices which have not yet been paid. If so, the financial coordinator should investigate the nonpayment of these invoices with the responsible staff member and make appropriate follow-up.

# Petty Cash

A maximum amount to be in petty cash fund must be set, depending on the size of the company. For example, a company may determine that the petty cash fund may not exceed $ 300. Usually, the financial coordinator is the custodian of the petty cash fund. Also, the maximum amount that can be disbursed from petty cash must be set. For example, a company must decide that a single disbursement from petty cash shall never exceed $50.00.

The petty cash fund should operate on an impress basis. Therefore, when it is time to replenish the petty cash fund, the financial coordinator should total out the expenses made and identify those expenses by general ledger account number. When the check request is submitted for payment it should indicate the total amount needed to bring the fund back up to the maximum amount. Also, the check request should breakdown the various expense accounts being charged and the amount charged to each.

Request for petty cash reimbursement should be listed on the Petty Cash Fund Reconciliation Sheet. A description of the item charged should be recorded together with the amount. A vendor receipt must be received for the amount of the request in order for the request to be approved. Any recipient of the petty cash funds should sign the sheet to indicate receipt of the funds. The paid receipt should be attached to the sheet. All paid information should be kept in the locked petty cash box until it is time to replenish the fund. The Petty Cash Fund Reconciliation Sheet and associated receipts are attached to the check request voucher at the time of replenishment. The petty cash box is to be locked at all times when the no disbursing or replenishing has been done.

At least once annually, the general manager or administrative manager should conduct a "surprise" review of the fund. When this is done, he/she should count, while the financial coordinator is in attendance, the total monies on hand and the total amount of receipts in the petty cash box. The two amounts should equal exactly the maximum amount of the petty cash fund. Any discrepancies should be discussed and resolved immediately.

## Bookkeeping, Banking, and Accounts Management

*Bookkeeping:* Bookkeeping is the systematic recording of business transactions. Some business managers hire a part time accountant to deal with all the accounting works for them. This is a choice. You may want to do it yourself. Whether you hire a consultant or do it yourself, there are basic accounting principles that you need to understand. There are basic bookkeeping works that you will still have to do. For example, you will have to record cash received, cash disbursed, sales, purchases, payroll, equipment, inventory, accounts receivable, and accounts payable. Usually, a set of books of accounts includes four journals and one ledger. The four journals are:

- *Sales journal* used to record all sales on accounts,
- *Cash journal* used to record cash received and cash paid,
- *Purchase journal* used to record purchases on accounts,
- And the *general journal* used for any transaction that cannot be entered either as sales, cash or purchase.

The *ledger* is a book that includes all the accounts (cash, merchandise purchases, expenses, investment, furniture, merchandise inventory, merchandise sales, notes receivables, notes payables, etc). Actually, the transactions that have been entered in the journals are posted or copied to their respective accounts (pages) in the ledger.

Each month the financial coordinator and administrative manager should review the ending balance shown on balance sheet accounts such as the cash accounts, accounts receivable, accounts payable and deferred revenue. The financial coordinator and administrative manager should review the bank reconciliations, schedules of accounts receivable and deferred revenue and the aging of accounts payable to support the balances shown on the balance sheet.

*Banking:* In addition to bookkeeping, you will have to deal with banking. In other words, you will possibly have to write checks, accept checks, endorse checks, make deposits, reconcile bank statements, and make electronic banking transactions. Best practice is to handle personal expenses in a separate checking account.

Also, you should make monthly bank statement reconciliation to ensure consistency and accuracy, by comparing records from your book with statements received from the bank. After review of bank statements is conducted, the general manager or the administrative manager should initial and date the bottom, right hand corner of the first page of each bank statement reviewed. The reviewed bank statement should then be forwarded to the financial coordinator (an individual without check signing rights) to reconcile the bank accounts using the approved reconciliation form. All accounts should be reconciled in a timely manner, usually no later than 7 days after receipt of the monthly bank statements. In the event it is not possible to reconcile the bank statements in this period of time, the general manager or administrative manager should be notified by a written memo from the financial coordinator. When reconciling the bank accounts, it is important to consider the following:

- Comparison of dates and amounts of daily deposits on the bank statements with the cash receipts journal.
- Investigation of items rejected by the bank (returned checks or deposits).
- Comparison of wire transfers, dates received with dates sent.
- Comparison of canceled checks with the disbursement journal as to check number, payee and amount.
- An examination of canceled checks for authorized signatures, irregular endorsements, and alterations.
- Review of void checks.
- Investigation and administrative decision on all outstanding checks for more than six months.

## Purchasing and Assets Management

Obviously, purchase is a critical issue of financial management. If you do not manage your purchase practices carefully, this can affect your profit. Before making any purchase,

- ensure that you specify your needs with details,
- have quotes from more than one vendor or service provider,
- issue a purchase order, so you can avoid being charged for the wrong product or service.

A receipt from the vendor detailing every individual good or service purchased accompanied by an explanation of the specific business purpose which was furthered by each expenditure. For example, "Round trip coach flight Tampa to Atlanta for Team Leader Nancy Orman to participate in annual conference of financial planners".

Many companies require that three bids be obtained before any purchasing decision be made for all major expenditures such as computers, furniture, audit services, printing services, and other similar services. All bids, including phone quotes, must be recorded and kept on file. Purchases that involve contracts with consultants should include justification for payment, rate and schedule of pay, deliverables, time frame, and other information such as work plan.

The financial coordinator should maintain a permanent property log or database for all fixed assets purchased by a company. The log should contain the following information:

- Date of purchase
- Description of item purchased
- Cost or fair market value on the date receipt
- Identification/serial number (if appropriate)
- Depreciation period
- Vendor name and address
- Warranty period
- Inventory tag number (all fixed assets should be tagged with a unique identifying number)
- Number of the company check used to pay for the equipment

Physical inspection and inventory should be taken of a small business fixed assets and reconciled to the general ledger balances. This can be done at least on an annual basis. Any material changes in the status of property and equipment should be documented.

## Credit and Financing

*Credit:* In the matter of business, credit is a burning issue of financial management. I am not talking about credit for your business. I mean credit that you extend to clients when they purchase goods or services from your business. You need to set policies for how you will extend credit to customers and how you will collect your money. As much as you can, avoid bringing people to court to collect money. Make sure that you respect the laws when you attempt to make a money collection. Do not threaten customers or verbally abuse them in any way. Keep it polite, but firm. Communication and negotiation of how you can collect your money is a key strategy.

*Financing:* Most small businesses prosper through the benefits of loans. You can receive loans from individuals, banks, and government. Leasing equipment is also another way to finance your business. But keep in mind that most banks will not finance small businesses that are less than two years old. They will want to see your recent tax returns, financial statements, and cash flow projections. Also, they may not loan you more than 50% of your business capitalization. The Small Business Administration (SBA) usually considers loan requests from business that failed to receive loan from banks. Of course, there is more paper work to deal with. Also, the time to get approval may be longer.

The Small Business Administration (SBA) is a federal agency established in 1953 to provide assistance to American small business in a wide range of areas, including, but not limited to, advocacy, financial assistance, management, and procurement. The SBA offers three basic types of loan programs:
- The section 7(a) Loan Guaranty Program;
- The section 504 Certified Development Company (CDC) Program;
- The Micro Loan, a section 7(m) Loan Program.

The basic section 7(a) Loan Guaranty Program helps qualified startup and existing small businesses that were unsuccessful in obtaining a loan from regular lending institutions. The small business applies through a lender (bank) that participates in the SBA programs, not directly through SBA. Usually, the loan is available for small businesses in: (a) agricultural industries (up to $.5 million), construction (average three years annual sales or receipt, up to $ 28.5 million), manufacturing and mining (of not more than 500 employees), retail or service (three year annual sales, up to $29 million), special trade contractors (up to $ 7 million), and wholesale (of not more than 100 employees). The Basic 7(a) SBA loans can be used for furniture and fixture, land and buildings, machinery and equipment, tenant improvements under lease agreement, working capital, and even refinancing prior debt. The loans can be for periods of up to 10 years for working capital and up to 25 years for fixed asset financing.

The section 504 Certified Development Company (CDC) Program aims at financing the acquisition of real estate, machinery, or equipment for expansion or modernization of a small business. The 504 loans are for small businesses with tangible net worth that does not exceed $7.5 million and average net income of $2.5 million after taxes for the preceding two years.

The Micro Loan, a section 7(m) Loan Program provides short-term loans of up to $35,000 to small businesses and non-profit child care centers. These loans can be used for furniture, fixtures, machinery and/or equipment, purchasing inventory, supplies, and working capital.

As said earlier, a small business becomes eligible for SBA loans after being turned down by a commercial lender. The SBA does not make loans. It guarantees loans made by commercial lenders that participate in the SBA's Loan Guarantee Plan. Small businesses still have to meet some criteria such as good credit history, vested interest (equity invested in the business), adequate working capital, ability to repay (personal assets and liabilities, personal tax returns for the past three years, balance sheets for the past three years, accounts receivables and payable aging), and experience of the business owner. Obviously, there must be a well written business plan, including:

- balance sheets from the last three years,
- profit and loss statements from the last three years,
- cash flow projection,
- Accounts receivable and payable aging,
- Articles of incorporation,
- Leases,
- Proof of insurance for collateralized items,
- Equipment inventories,
- And other similar documents that may vary from one lender to another.

Small businesses have some other financing options. The most current are credit cards and line of credit. A credit card is offered based on personal and business credit history. Some lenders offer credit cards with additional discount features (hotels, gas, car rental, travel insurance, etc) that may help save some money.

Unlike the credit card, a line of credit is a semi-loan, which provides the option to withdraw money as needed, up to a specified borrowing limit. The borrower can pay back previous expenses and withdraw money as long as the borrowing limit is not exceeded. It is a revolving loan. There is basically no fixed terms. It is like a continuing source of finance for which the borrower does not need to re-apply each time funds are needed. The interest is usually lower for a line of credit than a credit card. The line of credit is based on the borrower credit worthiness and income potential. The line of credit can be used for inventory purchase, short-term working capital needs, and other operating expenses as necessary.

## Taxes

A small business is affected by federal, state, and local tax systems. As a small business entrepreneur, you have to be aware of that. To some extent, managing tax issues is closely related to your record keeping system. You need to keep record of income and expenses as well as the tax tables published by the Internal Revenue Service. It is important to meet your tax obligations. In fact, there are taxes and fees that you pay up front to operate your business, such as business license, incorporation or partnership registration, professional registration, trade name registration, zoning permits, business permits, mailing permits, etc. However, there are other taxes that you pay:

a) either quarterly:
- Estimated income tax deposits,
- Income tax withholding deposits,
- FICA tax deposits,
- FUTA tax deposits;

b) or annually:
- Income tax,
- Income tax withholding,
- Self-employment tax,

- FICA tax,
- FUTA tax.

The IRS requires to retain tax records for up to three years after a tax return is filed. Always check with the Internal Revenue Services (IRS) to inquire about all taxes related to your business, either by phone or through their website (www.irs.gov).

The following are tax calendars for which sole proprietorship, partnership, S corporation, and C Corporation businesses may be liable:

**Figure 22**
**Tax Calendar for which Sole Proprietorship, Partnership, S Corporation, and C Corporation Businesses may be Liable**

| Month | Date | Tax | Forms |
|---|---|---|---|
| January | 15 | Estimated tax | Form 1040ES |
| | 31 | Social security (FICA) tax and the withholding of income tax (See IRS rulings for deposit – Pub. 334) | Forms 941, 941E, 942, and 943. |
| | 31 | Providing information on social security (FICA)tax and the withholding of income tax | Form W-2 (to employee) |
| | 31 | Federal unemployment (FUTA) tax | Form 940-EZ or 940 |
| | 31 | Federal unemployment (FUTA) tax (only if liability for unpaid taxes exceeds $100) | Form 8109 (to make deposit) |
| | 31 | Information returns to non-employees and transactions with other persons | Form 1099 (to recipient) |

| February | 28 | Information returns to non-employees and transactions with other persons | Form 1099 (to IRS) |
|---|---|---|---|
| | 28 | Providing information on social security (FICA)tax and the withholding of income tax | Forms W-2 and W-3 (to Social Security Adm.) |
| April | 15 | Income tax | Schedule C (Form 1040) |
| | 15 | Self-employment tax | Schedule SE (Form 1040) |
| | 15 | Estimated tax | Form 1040ES |
| | 30 | Social security (FICA) tax and the withholding of income tax (See IRS rulings for deposit – Pub. 334) | Forms 941, 941E, 942, and 943 |
| | 30 | Federal unemployment (FUTA) tax (only if liability for unpaid taxes exceeds $100) | Form 8109 (to make deposits) |
| June | 15 | Estimated tax | Form 1040ES |
| July | 31 | Social security (FICA) tax and the withholding of income tax (See IRS rulings for deposit – Pub. 334) | Forms 941, 941E, 942, and 943 |
| | 31 | Federal unemployment (FUTA) tax (only if liability for unpaid taxes exceeds $100) | Form 8109 (to make deposits) |
| September | 15 | Estimated tax | Form 1040ES |

| October | 31 | Social security (FICA) tax and the withholding of income tax (See IRS rulings for deposit – Pub. 334) | Forms 941, 941E, 942, and 943 |
|---------|-----|-----|-----|
|  | 31 | Federal unemployment (FUTA) tax (only if liability for unpaid taxes exceeds $100) | Form 8109 (to make deposits) |

If your tax year is not January 1st through December 31st,
- Schedule C (Form 1040) is dues the 15th day of the 4th month after end of the tax year.
- Schedule E is due same day as Form 1040.

Estimated tax (1040ES) is due the 15th day of 4th, 6th, and 9th months of tax year, and the 15th day of 1st month after the end of tax year.

# Payroll

Generating the payroll for your business involves the following:
- You have hired employees. You cannot have payroll without employees.
- You obtained an Employer Identification Number (EIN) or tax identification number from the Internal Revenue Service (Form SS-4).
- Each employee has filed and signed the Employee's Withholding Allowance Certificate (Form W-4).
- You have employees' information sheets.
- You have an IRS tax table.
- You calculate the employees' earnings.
- You subtract the taxes and other deductions.
- You write the paychecks.
- You create employees' earning records.
- You prepare you payroll register.
- You submit your payroll taxes.

*Employee Payroll Information Sheet*: A payroll information sheet must be prepared for each employee, and include the following information:
- Employee identification number,
- Last name and first name of the employee,
- Earning to date,
- Hourly rate,
- Regular work hours
- Overtime hours (if any),
- Overtime earning (if any),
- Total gross pay,
- Earning subject to unemployment,
- Earning subject to FICA,
- Social Security/Medicare(FICA),
- Federal withholding,
- State withholding,
- Health insurance,
- Net pay,
- And check number.

The following is a template to record employees' earnings:

**Figure 23**
**Sample Payroll Register Template**

Pay Period From _____ To _____

| Emp.# | Last Name | First Name | E.t.d. | H.R. | R.H. | OTH | OTE | G.E. | ESU | ESF | SSFICA | Med | F W/H | S W/H | HI | NP | Check # |
|-------|-----------|------------|--------|------|------|-----|-----|------|-----|-----|--------|-----|-------|-------|----|----|---------|
|  |  |  |  |  |  |  |  |  |  |  |  |  |  |  |  |  |  |
|  |  |  |  |  |  |  |  |  |  |  |  |  |  |  |  |  |  |
|  |  |  |  |  |  |  |  |  |  |  |  |  |  |  |  |  |  |
|  |  |  |  |  |  |  |  |  |  |  |  |  |  |  |  |  |  |
|  |  |  |  |  |  |  |  |  |  |  |  |  |  |  |  |  |  |
|  |  |  |  |  |  |  |  |  |  |  |  |  |  |  |  |  |  |
|  |  |  |  |  |  |  |  |  |  |  |  |  |  |  |  |  |  |
|  |  |  |  |  |  |  |  |  |  |  |  |  |  |  |  |  |  |
|  |  |  |  |  |  |  |  |  |  |  |  |  |  |  |  |  |  |
|  |  |  |  |  |  |  |  |  |  |  |  |  |  |  |  |  |  |
|  |  |  |  |  |  |  |  |  |  |  |  |  |  |  |  |  |  |
|  |  |  |  |  |  |  |  |  |  |  |  |  |  |  |  |  |  |

Notice:
Emp.# = Employment number
E.t.d. = Earnings to date
H.R. = Hourly Rate
R.H. = Regular Hours
O.T.H. = Over Time Hours
O.T.E. = Over Time Earnings
G.E. = Gross Earnings
E.S.U. = Earnings Subject to Unemployment
E.S.F. = Earnings Subject to FICA
S.S.FICA = Social Security FICA
Med. = Medicare
F.W/H = Federal Withholdings
S.W/H = State Withholdings
H.I. = Health Insurance
N.P. = Net Pay

*Employment-related taxes*: Employment-related taxes are taxes that an employer has to pay to the government as a result of hiring people to operate a business. Some of the taxes are deducted from employees. Some others are employer's contributions. Employment-related taxes are income taxes, social security/ Medicare, unemployment compensation insurance, and workers' compensation.

*Income taxes*: Income taxes are withheld from each employee's earning during each pay period, based on (a) each employee's total wages, (b) number of exemptions claimed on form W-4, (c) marital status, (d) and length of pay period. Every quarter, employer must submit to the IRS the amount withheld along with Form 941. At the end of each taxable year, employer must complete form W-2, wages and tax statement, and mail it to the employee by January 31. The Circular E., Employer's Tax Guide published by the IRS will provide you with detailed information on taxes.

*Social Security/Medicare Taxes*: The Social Security/Medicare or Federal Insurance Contributions Act (FICA)taxes are taxes that employers are required to withhold from each employee (about 6.2%), match with the same percentage, and pay to the government.

*Unemployment Compensation Insurance*: Unemployment Compensation Insurance includes two parts. The first part is a federal tax that an employer contributes for each employee. This is not a deduction from the employee's earnings. The amount that the employer pays is based on the employee earnings. The second part is determined differently by each state.

*Worker's Compensation or Employer's Annual Federal Unemployment (FUTAX) tax return*: Employers are required to provide their employees with workers' compensation against possible loss of income that results from work-related injury, disease, or disability. It is usually purchased through an insurance program.

## Financial Reporting

*Financial Statements:* Bookkeeping records will be used to produce financial statements, which are, but not limited to:
- *Income Statement:* A comparative summary of all revenues as well as operating expenses for a business during a month, a quarter, or a year, or any given period;
- *Cash flow statement:* A summary that shows the availability of cash to cover expenses, invest or take as profits;
- *Balance sheet:* A summary of the overall financial condition of a business at the close of an accounting period.

## Budgeting

You had a budget in your business plan. Since you are dealing with the concrete now, you will probably have to make some adjustments in your budget, so it can help as a tool to monitor profits for your business. Every fiscal year, you have to budget for your business. A budget is a plan that sets financial goals (usually to increase profit) and indicates the steps to achieve these goals. When you are setting financial goals for your business,
- Assess your fixed and variable expenses,

- Set financial goal for net profit after tax,
- Compare revenue and costs,
- Calculate your return on investment.

| **DO IT YOURSELF!** |
|---|
| 1. How do you think good financial management practices can help grow your business? |

2. Make a payroll for the first three months of the opening of your business.

3. You are about to make the budget for the next fiscal year. Indicate a list of documents that you will need for effective budgeting and what information that you will diligently look for these documents.

# CHAPTER VIII
## Financial Analysis

As indicated earlier, assets represent anything of value that belongs to a company while liabilities encompass anything that is owed by a company. Anything that is owned exclusively by a company is called equity. Also, as seen previously, the balance sheet is a snapshot of the financial position of a company at a specific point in time, generally at the close of an accounting period. On the other hand, the income statement shows the income generated and the expenses incurred by a company over a period of time. This chapter introduces some basic formula using the information provided by the balance sheet and the income statement, which will enable a small business owner or manager to make selected financial analyses of the level of profitability, liquidity, solvency, efficiency, and growth of a company.

## Profitability

Simply put, profitability refers to the surplus of revenue over expenses. The gross profit margin, the net profit margin, the return on assets, and the return on equity are four examples of financial ratios to assess the profitability of a small business.

*Gross Profit margin*

The gross profit margin helps measure how a company uses its revenues and controls its expenses to generate acceptable rate of return. The profit margin is calculated by dividing the "sales less cost of goods sold" by sales. The gross profit margin calculates the percentage of profit that a company generates for every dollar in sales.

Gross profit margin = Sales less cost of goods sold / sales x 100.

*Example:*

The following information were found in STAR RETAIL STORE, INC. income statement for the year ended December 31, 2004:

Sales less cost of goods sold: $50,000
Sales: $80,000

Calculate the gross profit margin!

*Solution:*

Gross profit margin = $50,000/$80,000 x 100

Gross profit margin = 62.5 %

*Interpretation:*

The gross profit margin of Star retail store is 62.5%. In other words, Star retail store makes 62.5 cents of gross profit for every dollar in sales. This gross profit margin must be compared with the industry average profit margin to determine whether it is lower or higher.

*Net profit margin*

The Net profit margin measures the profitability of a company after all deductions (taxes, operating expenses) have been made. The net profit margin is calculated by dividing the earning after taxes or the net profit by sales.

Net profit margin = Earnings after taxes (Net profit) / Sales x 100

*Example:*

The following information were found in ABEL CORPORATION income statement for the year ended December 31, 2006:

Sales: $ 2,200,000
Earnings after taxes: $ 166,000

Calculate the net profit margin!

*Solution:*

Net profit margin = Earnings after taxes/Sales

Net profit margin = $166,000 / $ 2,200,000 x 100

Net profit margin = 7%

*Interpretation:*

The net profit margin of ABEL CORPORATION is 7%. ABEL CORPORATION makes a net profit of 7 cents on every dollar in sales. As for the gross profit margin, this net profit margin must be compared with the industry average profit margin to determine whether it is lower or higher.

*Return on assets (ROA)*

The return on assets is a measure of the return on the total investment of an organization. The ROA is computed by dividing the net profit by total assets.

ROA = Net profit/Total assets x 100

*Example:*

The following information were found in Good Taste Restaurant income statement and balance sheet.

Net profit: $ 60,000
Total assets: $ 900,000

Calculate the return on assets (ROA)!

*Solution:*

ROA = $60,000 / $ 900,000 x 100
ROA = 6.66%

*Interpretation:*

Good Taste restaurant generates 6.66% return on the assets that it utilizes in its operations.

*Return on equity (ROE)*

The Return on Equity Ratio (ROE) measures the profitability in relation to equity fund or ownership. The return on equity is calculated by dividing the earnings after taxes (or net profit) by equity. A ratio over 20% is considered attractive.

Return on equity = Earnings after taxes (Net profit)/Equity x 100
*Example:*

The following information were found in Good Taste Restaurant income statement and balance sheet:

Earnings after taxes or Net profit: $ 116,000
Equity: $ 485,000

Calculate the return on equity (ROE)!

*Solution:*

Return on equity = Earnings after taxes or Net profit/ Equity
Return on equity = $116,000/$485,000 x 100
Return on equity = 34%

*Interpretation:*

Good Taste Restaurant generates 34% return on the capital invested by its owners.

# Liquidity

Liquidity is the ability to meet cash requirements (e.g. paying bills). Examples of measures of liquidity include the current ratio, the acid test, acid test ratio, the inventory turnover, the receivable turnover, and the average collection period.

*Current ratio*

The current ratio helps measure the ability to pay the bills on time. It is calculated by dividing the total current assets by the total current liabilities. In other words, the current ratio calculates how many dollars in assets are likely to be converted into cash within a period of one year to enable a company to pay its debts during that same year.

Current ratio = total current assets/ total current liabilities

*Example:*

The following information were found in JAF Company income statement and balance sheet, December 31, 2004.

Current assets: $250,000

Current liabilities: $200,000

Calculate the current ratio!

*Solution:*

|  (1)<br>Year End Current Assets /<br>$250,000 / |  (2)<br>Current Liab.<br>$200,000 |  (1)/(2)<br>Current Ratio<br>1.25 |
|---|---|---|

*Interpretation:*

JAF has $1.25 of Current Assets to meet $1.00 of its Current Liability. A current ratio of assets to liabilities of 2:1 is usually considered to be acceptable (e.g. your current assets are twice your current liabilities).

*Net working capital (NWC)*

The net working capital measures the ability of an organization to face unforeseen expenses. It is calculated by subtracting the current liabilities from the current assets.

NWC = Current assets – Current liabilities

*Example:*

The balance sheet of MRC Company provides the following information for June 30, 2001:

Current assets: $ 48,000
Current liabilities: $ 21,000

Calculate the working capital!

*Solution*

NWC = Current assets – Current liabilities

NWC = $48,000 - $ $21,000

NWC = $ 27,000

*Interpretation:*

The current assets of MRC company exceeded its current liabilities by $ 27,000 in June 30, 2001. In other words, MRC company has a positive net working capital to weather an unforeseen financial crisis.

Note: The net working capital (NWC) and the current Ratio (CR) serve the same purpose. The difference is that the NWC refers to an amount of cash or near-cash asset whereas the CR is ratio.

*Quick (Acid-Test) Ratio (QR)*

The Acid-test or quick ratio or liquid ratio measures the ability of an organization to use its near cash or quick assets to immediately pay its current liabilities. A Quick Ratio of 1 or more will enable an organization to pay back its current liabilities; whereas, a company with quick ratio of less than 1, cannot currently pay back its current liabilities.

The higher the ratio, the greater the company's liquidity (i.e., the better able to meet current obligations using liquid assets).

$$QR = \frac{\text{Current Assets - Inventory}}{\text{Current Liabilities}}$$

*Example:*

The following information were found in JAF company balance sheet, December 31, 2001:
Current assets: $100,000
Inventory: $ 40,000
Current liabilities: $50,000

Calculate the quick ratio!

*Solution*

Quick Ratio = ($100,000 - $40,000) / $50,000
QR=$60,000/$50,000
QR= 1.2

*Interpretation:*

JAF has $ 1.2 of quick cash for every dollar it owes. Ideally, quick ratio should be 1:1. A quick ratio higher than 1:1 indicates that the business can meet its current financial obligations with the available quick funds on hand. A quick ratio lower than 1:1 may indicate that the company relies too much on inventory or other assets to pay its short-term liabilities. Many lenders are interested in this ratio because it does not include inventory, which may or may not be easily converted into cash.

# Efficiency

Efficiency refers to how well a company manages its overall assets and liabilities. Accounts payable turnover, inventory turnover, accounts receivable turnover, and average collection period are four examples of ratios that can help analyze the ability of a company to meet short and long term obligations.

*Accounts payable turnover*

The accounts payable turnover measures the percentage of company sales that is being funded by its suppliers. The accounts payable turnover is obtained by dividing the accounts payable by net sales.

Accounts payables turnover = [Accounts payables / Net sales] x 100

*Example:*

The following information were found in the balance sheet and income statement of Raimbow Corporation:
Accounts payable: $ 150,000
Net sales: $ 400,000
Calculate the accounts payable turnover ratio!

*Solution*

Accounts Payables to Sales Ratio = [$150,000/$400, 000] x 100
Accounts Payables to Sales Ratio = 37.05%

*Interpretation:*

37.05% of Rainbow Corporation sales are being funded by its suppliers.

*Inventory turnover*

The inventory turnover measures the number of days it takes for a company to turn inventory into cash (cash sales) or an accounts receivable (credit sales). Inventory is a percentage of current assets. Inventory can help determine whether an "excessive" buildup of inventory contributes to a liquidity problem. Inventory turnover is calculated in dividing the "Cost of goods sold" by "Inventory". If information about "Cost of goods sold" is not available, the data for "Sales" can be used.

Inventory turnover = Cost of goods sold/ Inventory

*Example:*

The following information were found in the income statement of HAPPY FACE DAY CARE:

Cost of goods sold: $ 300, 000
Inventory: $ 75,000

Calculate the inventory turnover!

*Solution:*

Inventory turnover = Cost of goods sold/ Inventory

Inventory turnover = $300,000 / $75,000

Inventory turnover = 4 times

*Interpretation:*

Happy Face Day Care is able to rotate its inventory in sales 4 times in one fiscal year. Note! If high inventory becomes a problem, a company may decide to use the Just In Time (JIT) approach. Simply put, the JIT consists of adopting a policy to purchase materials and produce units as customer demands arise. This enables a company to reduce inventory to the strict minimum or even to zero. Also, resources that were previously used for inventory can be reallocated for continuous improvement of the company or to increase profit.

*Accounts Receivable Turnover:*

The accounts receivable turnover helps determine the number of times accounts receivable are paid and reestablished during the accounting period. The accounts receivable turnover is obtained by dividing the annual credit sales by accounts receivable. The higher the turnover, the faster the business is collecting its receivables and the more cash the client generally has on hand.

Accounts receivable turnover = Annual credit sales/Accounts receivable

*Example:*

Annual credit sales: $ 240,000
Accounts receivable: $ 80,000

*Solution:*

Accounts receivable turnover = $240,000 / $20,000
Accounts receivable turnover = 12 times

*Interpretation:*

ABC store collects accounts receivable 12 times a year. This turnover must be compared with other companies of the same size.

*Accounts Receivable Collection Period:*

The accounts receivable collection period is calculated to determine how many days it takes a company to collect all accounts receivable. The accounts receivable collection is obtained by dividing 360 days of the year (12 months of 30 days) by the accounts receivable turnover.

Accounts receivable collection period = 360 days/Accounts receivable turnover

*Example:*

Annual credit sales: $ 240,000
Accounts receivable: $ 80,000

*Solution:*

*Step 1:* Calculate account receivable turnover
Accounts receivable turnover = $240,000 / $20,000
Accounts receivable turnover = 12 times
*Step 2:* Calculate average collection period
Average collection period = 360 days/Accounts receivable turnover
Average collection period = 360 / 12
Average collection period = 30 days

*Interpretation:*

ABC store collects credit sales every 30 days. This average collection must be compared to that of other industries of similar size to determine whether this company is more or less efficient.

## Solvency or leverage

Solvency is the ability to pay all debts if the business was sold tomorrow. Some of the measures of solvency are the debt ratio, and the debt-to-equity ratio.

*Debt ratio*

The debt ratio is used to measure the ability to pay all debts if the organization was sold tomorrow. It is calculated in dividing the total liabilities by the total assets. The debt ratio calculates the long term solvency of a company. The total debt ratio should be 1 or less. A company with a high debt ratio is in danger of becoming insolvent, and risks to going bankrupt.

Debt ratio = Total liabilities / Total assets

*Example:*

The following information were found in JAF corporation balance sheet, December 31, 2002

Liabilities: $150,000

Assets: $ 300,000

Calculate the debt ratio!

*Solution*

Debt ratio = $150,000 / $300,000 = 0.50 or 50%

*Interpretation:*

50% of assets have been financed by debt.

*Debt to Equity (Fund balance) ratio (DER)*

The debt to equity ratio measures the proportion of long-term debt to common equity or fund balance. The DER is calculated by dividing the long-term debt by equity.

DER = Long-term debt/Equity

*Example:*

The following information were found in MLF Corporation balance sheet, December 31, 2000
Liabilities: $200,000
Fund balance or equity: $ 150,000
Calculate the Debt to Equity (Fund balance) ratio

*Solution:*

DER = $200,000/ $ 150,000
DER = 1.33

*Interpretation:*

MLF has $1.33 cents of Debt and only $1.00 in Equity to meet this obligation.
Or
For every dollar of equity financing, MLF uses $1.33 of long-term debt.
Or
MLF owes $1.33 for every dollar it owns.

# Financial growth

Financial growth is the measure of the percentage increase in the financial operations of a company in comparison to a previous period. A company may be expanding without any substantial financial growth. One of the best strategies to analyze a company financial growth is to determine the internal financial trends and compare them with companies of the same profile. The percentage change and the common size ratios are to examples of measure of financial growth analysis.

*Percentage change*

Percentage change is the calculation of the percentage of change from one year to another in line items of financial statements (balance sheet, income statement, statement of cash flow).

Rules to calculate percentage change:

1. Calculate the difference between the number for period "A" (most recent period) and the number for period "B" (preceding period).
2. Divide the difference by the number for period "A".
3. Multiply the result by 100.

*Example:*

The balance sheet of JAF for 2004 and 2005 reflect the following cash information:

2005 2004
Cash $20,000 $24,000

What is the percentage change from 2004 to 2005?

*Solution:*

1. Calculate the difference between the number for period "A" and the number for period "B".

"A" – "B" = $20,000 - $ 24,000 = - $4,000

2. Divide the difference by the number for period "A".

-$4,000 / $20,000 = - .20

3. Multiply the result by 100.

-.20 x 100 = 20%

*Interpretation:*

From 2004 to 2005, JAF has recorded a 20% decrease in cash.

*Common size ratios (CSR)*

Common size ratios are used to compare trends in financial statements of an organization over time or to compare the financial situations of various organizations with similar profiles. The common size ratio for a line item is calculated by dividing the item of interest by the reference item.

*3.1. For assets:*

Common size = asset of interest / Total assets

*Example:*

Cash : $ 4,135
Total assets: $18,056

Calculate common size ratio for cash!

*Solution:*

Common size cash = $4,135/$18,056 = 0.23
Multiplied by 100

Common size cash = $4,135/$18,056 = 23%

*3.2. For liabilities*

Common size = Liabilities of interest/Total assets

*Example:*

Accounts payable: $1,553
Total liabilities and fund balance: $18,056
Calculate common size ratio for accounts payable!

*Solution:*

Common size accounts payable = $1,553/$18,056 =0.09

Multiplied by 100

Common size accounts payable = 9%

*3.3. For Income or revenue*

Common size = Income of interest / Net sales

*Example:*

Cost of goods Sold: $2,000
Operating expenses: $100
Total revenue: $2,400
Calculate common size ratio for cost of goods sold, then for operating expenses!

*Solution:*

Common size Cost of goods Sold = $2,000 / $2,400 = 0.833

Multiplied by 100

Common size Cost of goods Sold = 83.3%

Common size Operating expenses = $100/$2,400 = 0.042

Multiplied by 100

Common size Operating expenses = 4.2%

**Figure 24**
**Sample Comparative Balance sheet and**
**Comparative Common size Balance Sheet**

| Assets | 2002 | % | 2003 | % |
|---|---|---|---|---|
| Current assets | | | | |
| Cash | $4,135 | 23% | $5,347 | 29% |
| Accounts receivable | 1,661 | 9% | 1,188 | 6% |
| Inventory | 2,546 | 14% | 2,674 | 14% |
| Notes receivable | 1,950 | 11% | 1,114 | 6% |
| Total current assets | $10,292 | 57% | $10,323 | 56% |
| Long –term assets | | | | |
| Land building and equipment | 6,283 | 35% | 7,074 | 38% |
| Vehicle | 1,481 | 8% | 1,170 | 6% |
| Total long-term assets | 7,764 | 43% | 8,244 | 44% |
| Total assets | $18,056 | 100% | $18,567 | 100% |
| | | | | |

| Liabilities and Equity | | | | |
|---|---|---|---|---|
| Current liabilities | | | | |
| Accounts payable | $1,553 | 9% | $2,432 | 13% |
| Notes payable | 1,228 | 7% | 1,318 | 7% |
| Acquisition contracts | 11,935 | 66% | 6,202 | 33% |
| Total current liabilities | $14,716 | 82% | $9,952 | 54% |
| Long-term liabilities | | | | |
| Notes payable | 5,543 | 31% | 1,504 | 8% |
| Deferred credits | 36 | 0% | 0 | |
| Total long-term liabilities | 5,579 | 31% | 1,504 | 8% |
| Total liabilities | 20,295 | 112% | 11,456 | 62% |
| Equity | -2,239 | -12% | 7,111 | 38% |
| Total liabilities and Equity | $18,056 | 100% | $18,567 | 100% |

Figure 25
Sample income statement and common
size ratio income statement
Loving hand retail store,
Year Ended December 31

| | 2008 | % | 2007 | % |
|---|---|---|---|---|
| Net Sales | 2 400 | 100.0% | 1800 | 100.0% |
| Cost of Goods Sold | 2 000 | 83.3% | 1400 | 77.8% |
| Gross Margin on Sales | 400 | 16.7% | 400 | 22.2% |
| Operating Expenses | 100 | 4.2% | 80 | 4.4% |
| Net Income | 300 | 12.5% | 320 | 17.8% |

| DO IT YOURSELF |
| --- |

## Harry Computing Center, Inc. (HCC)

The Harry Computing Center (HCC) is based in Houston, Texas. The mission of OCF is to provide quality copying and computing services to the clients in the Houston area. Prior to the annual board of directors meeting, the following financial statements (Balance sheet and income statement) were distributed to all members.

The standard ratios for companies with the size of HCC are the following:

- Current ratio: 2.2
- Quick ratio: 1.3
- Working capital: $80,000
- Return on assets: 35%
- Return on equity: 10%

Questions

You are a member of an ad-hoc committee that must answer the following questions, using the information from the balance sheet and income statement:

1. Do the financial statements of HCC provide indicators of organizational growth? Explain!

2. Do you think HCC has the ability to pay its bills on time? Explain!

3. Do you think that HCC has become more solvent or less solvent? Explain!

4. What factors account for increase or decrease in HCC solvency?

6. Would you conclude that HCC is a relatively profitable, solvent, efficient company, which is financially growing? Explain!

7. What would be your financial management recommendations to HCC board for the next fiscal year?

## Harry Computing Center (HCC)
## Balance sheet December 31, 2003, and 2004

| | | 2004 | 2003 |
|---|---|---|---|
| ASSETS | | | |
| | Current assets | | |
| | Cash | $ 95,000.00 | $ 85,000.00 |
| | Account receivables | $ 50,000.00 | $ 80,000.00 |
| | Notes receivables | $ 150,000.00 | $100,000.00 |
| | Inventory | $ 350,000.00 | $325,000.00 |
| | Prepaid expenses | $ 30,000.00 | $ 35,000.00 |
| | Total current assets | $ 675,000.00 | $625,000.00 |
| | Fixed assets | | |
| | Investments | $ 100,000.00 | $ 75,000.00 |
| | Land, buildings, & equipment | $ 120,000.00 | $110,000.00 |
| | Vehicles | $ 75,000.00 | $ 55,000.00 |
| | Less: Accumulated depreciation | $ (20,000.00) | $ (15,000.00) |
| | Net equipment | $ 50,000.00 | $ 40,000.00 |
| | Total fixed assets | $ 325,000.00 | $265,000.00 |
| Total assets | | $ 1,000,000.00 | $890,000.00 |

| LIABILITIES AND EQUITY | | | |
|---|---|---|---|
| Current liabilities | | | |
| | Accounts payable | $ 80,000.00 | $ 70,000.00 |
| | Bank loan | $ 90,000.00 | $ 95,000.00 |
| | Acquisitions contracts | $ 125,000.00 | $100,000.00 |
| | Total current liabilities | $ 295,000.00 | $265,000.00 |
| Long-term liabilities | | | |
| | Notes payable | $ 135,000.00 | $125,000.00 |
| | Total long term liabilities | $ 135,000.00 | $125,000.00 |
| Total liabilities | | $ 430,000.00 | $390,000.00 |
| | | | |
| Equity | | | |
| | Current, unrestricted | $ 350,000.00 | $120,000.00 |
| | Current, restricted | $ 220,000.00 | $480,000.00 |
| Total equity | | $ 570,000.00 | $600,000.00 |
| | | | |
| Total liabilities and equity | $ 1,000,000.00 | $890,000.00 | |

Harry Computing Center (HCC)
Income statements for the year ending December 31, 2003 and 2004

|  | 2004 | 2003 |
|---|---|---|
| Revenues |  |  |
| Net sales | $500,000.00 | $470,000.00 |
| Cost of goods sold | $200,000.00 |  |
|  |  |  |
| Expenditures |  |  |
| Salaries and benefits | $230,000.00 | $200,000.00 |
| Advertising | $ 20,000.00 | $ 15,000.00 |
| Rent | $ 45,000.00 | $ 35,000.00 |
| Supplies | $ 30,000.00 | $ 20,000.00 |
| Insurance | $ 20,000.00 | $ 40,000.00 |
| Utilities | $ 24,000.00 | $ 18,000.00 |
| Miscellaneous | $ 12,000.00 | $  8,000.00 |
| Total expenditures | $381,000.00 | $336,000.00 |
|  |  |  |
| Net income | $119,000.00 | $134,000.00 |

# CHAPTER IX
## Information management

During recent decades, information has become a vital part in the life of individuals and businesses in the modern world. We always have to make decisions to survive on a day-to-day basis based on the information that we have. People fail to make good decisions because of a lack of information. The issue is not in the information itself, but in the ability to manage of information. As an entrepreneur, managing information has to be an everyday challenge for you. The challenge is to set a system that can help you collect easily the best suitable information to support the decisions that you are making. There is always tons of information surrounding us. There is always a mountain of obstacles when it comes to make the choice of information. Effective organization and management of information may be a very critical tool for an entrepreneur in that regard.

No matter what the size of your small business is, you need a computer and an information system to manage data such as purchase of goods and services, services to customers, timing of service processing, monitoring obligations to stakeholders, and performance evaluation.

## Information Management System

Businesses start and grow based on decisions made by entrepreneurs and managers. Decisions rely on information recorded, analyzed, and reported. The information must be housed into a structured data base that helps avoid redundant, expensive queering, and waste of time, money, and human capital. The best solution in that regard is the existence of an effective information management system.

A cohesive and integrated system of information delivery and analytics can help a business remain competitive in this new economy characterized by an increasingly dominant role of information technology.

If you are not a professional in management information system, my best advice to you is to hire a professional who can help you define a framework of guidelines, policies or practices, standards, and procedures that can be integrated into all aspects of your business. A consultant can be very expensive. However, there is a creative way to have an information system by offering internship opportunities to information technology students from community colleges, colleges, or universities in your area. The process is simple. Do some research to find out whether such opportunity exists at nearby post-secondary schools. Contact the chair or the coordinator of the program that you identified based on your needs, in order to inform them about your intention to provide non-paid internship positions for students. This can be done by phone or in writing. The choice is yours. It is your responsibility to make your case in a win-win manner so students and program coordinators can feel excited about your offer. Remember that some interns can be very motivated and may be able to make great contributions to your business. This is also a strategy that you can utilize for effective hiring practices in your business. Furthermore, I would advise you to encourage your interns with a small compensation if your budget permits you to afford that.

## An Effective Information Management System

An effective information management system is designed based on the vision, mission, goals, and objectives of the small business. It includes data related to indicators that can help determine whether a company is on the right track to deliver its promises. An effective information system must meet at least five criteria:

- *Accuracy*: There is an internal control and check of

information as well as a uniform procedure manual, which enables the production of accurate information.

- *Completeness*: Summarized information from the system provides pertinent data that can be considered as complete enough to inspire decision making.
- *Consistency*: The system provides reliable, consistent, and uniform information.
- *Relevance*: Information obtained from the system is relevant, appropriate, and trustworthy.
- *Timeliness*: The system must be able to receive, process, edit, summarize, and adjust information in a timely manner, according to the needs of the users of your business.

As prerequisites for your information system, you will need:
- High-powered desktops,
- Database technology,
- Specialized software (PeopleSoft, Peachtree, Oracle, Hyperion, ReportMart, or custom web applications such as ijournals or ibudgets),
- Network technology.

Also, you need a good website to promote, sell your products/services, and develop interactions with your customers. A good website provides your customers the opportunity to:
- Obtain as much information as possible about your products or services,
- Place orders online,
- Obtain all shipping information,
- Check order status,
- Use technical assistance,
- Provide comments or feedback about your products or services,
- Find information for their personal education (may be about life, finance, currents events, etc).

## Purchase of Goods and Services

Decisions to purchase goods and services by a small business cannot result from chance. They have to be made based on the best information available at the time. A culture of information-based decision making is certainly the appropriate path. A well designed and functioning information system can help you cut inventory costs by using the just in time (JIT) approach. Just-In-Time (JIT) is used to eliminate waste, improve productivity and quality assurance, and help avoid repetitive tasks. With a Just-in-time approach, you don't need to spend money for warehousing huge inventories. The information system can house a data base of providers or suppliers, turn around time, and other appropriate or relevant information, which can help you provide your service more effectively while avoiding unnecessary inventory costs.

## Service Processing and Customer Service

Whether a small business sells goods or services, there is still a service processing aspect that the manager must take into account for the future of the business. You may offer the best product in the world and not be able to deliver and survive in the market if your service processing system is not information – based. First of all, an information system may contribute to better relationships and communication between your business and your providers or suppliers, with respect to production information, pricing information, delivery schedules and technical assistance. Also, through your information system you can increase the level of your customer satisfaction, and consequently increase profitability. For example, you can integrate your information system into your website and offer an online network for your major customers. The network can be designed to gather feedback from customers and use the information obtained to improve your services. Such network can help you understand the position of your products or services on segment markets. This may enable you to determine whether you have to lower your prices or/and add service dimensions to offset a higher price.

## Monitoring and Performance Management

Business growth and expansion is an expression of performance. Performance may be an empty concept if it cannot be monitored and documented. Now, tell me how you will be able to document the performance of your business if you don't have a query and analysis system in place. Some small businesses cultivate the bad habit of collecting information only when it has been asked for. This is a huge mistake. This practice will not serve you to analyze patterns, trends, and events that could save your business from avoidable disaster. A good information management system is one of the tools that a small business can use to foster accountability at all levels.

## Reporting and Decision Making

The existence of an information management system makes the reporting and decision making process easier for a small business manager. There is no need for last minute information gathering, because the information is available for immediate use. Basically, a decision is a choice made among many options for actions. The classical decision making process consists of:

- Collecting available information related to an issue or a need,
- Developing and analyzing possible courses of action,
- Choosing one possible course of action,
- And finally, assessing past choices.

The information system of a small business is the most effective tool that an entrepreneur can use to make informed decision. There are at least three levels of decision making that you will be dealing with:

- *Strategic decisions*, which are usually long-term based, unstructured, very summarized, infrequent, and relying on both internal and external information;
- *Tactical decisions*, which are usually mid-term based, semi-structured, summarized, semi-frequent, and relying mostly on internal information;
- *And Operational decisions*, which are usually short-term based,

structured, detailed, frequent, and relying almost exclusively on internal information.

The strategic decisions are made when setting long-term goals and adopting policies. The tactical decisions are made during the implementation of strategic goals. The operational decisions are these made on a day-to-day basis. Whether you are making strategic, tactical, or operational decisions, your best bet is to use as much information as possible, which can be obtained from your information system. In fact, there is no better place to obtain appropriate information about your products or services, your providers or suppliers, and your customers. They play a significant role in most decisions that an entrepreneur has to make. Most of the decisions that you make will affect them one way or another.

## Evaluation and Quality Improvement

Information management helps business not only for reporting, query, and analysis, but also to make evaluation for continuing quality improvement.

An information system is a great tool for total quality management. This concept is used for a systematic approach based on a culture of high standardization in planning and operations, in order to provide the best quality of products and services to customers or clients.

An entrepreneur must commit to quality according to his/her dream, vision, and mission. This is the basis of advertising and marketing. This is the secret of creating a stable client base. Basically, quality means selling a product or service that meets or even exceeds established standards.

You can manage quality by:
- translating standards into specific indicators that are clear and non-equivocal,
- establishing gradual steps to control standards,
- creating learning teams for quality evaluation and ways for improvement,
- Making follow up on improvements.

The best way to achieve this end is to use your information as knowledge and a product that you re-invest into your business. Quality is a key investment in attracting new clients or customers, and consequently in securing profits for your business.

## Budgeting and Planning

Budgeting and planning are two key activities in the life of a small business. They cannot be performed without the analysis of accurate and credible information. The planning process of a small business usually sets the stage for defining overall direction and goals that a company wants to achieve. This includes profitability goals, which should be part of the budget. In fact, budgeting is one aspect of planning. Likewise, a business planning cannot be completed without identifying the available and needed resources to implement the goals set. This is the role of budgeting to coordinate resources, production, and expenditures based on existing data and anticipation of the future.

Effective budgeting and planning must rely on accurate, timely, and useful reports, which could be generated from the information system. The system must be reliable in order to provide information that can inspire sound budgeting and planning decisions.

## DO IT YOURSELF!

1. Explain to a skeptical partner why you need an information system for your company.

2. Who will be the users of your information system?

3. What information that each category of users will need from the system? What are the decisions that it will facilitate them to make?

# CHAPTER X
## Risk management

Entrepreneurs start their small business to make a profit. Uncertainty and unforeseen circumstances can challenge the potentiality of a company to provide the expected profits. In other words, starting a business involves risks. Risks include (a) Possible loss such as fire, death, liability judgment that can deeply damage your business, (b) security problems such as door locks defection, insecure equipment, work injuries, and lack of information backup system, (c) crimes such as armed robbery, and employee theft. Doing business is taking risks. A manager must be aware of this fact, and decide how much uncertainty is unavoidable, and how much can be controlled through risk management. You can take risks wisely by adopting risk management practices.

## What is Risk Management?

Risk management is a structured approach to assess the threats to a business, develop strategies to control the risks associated with the identified threats, and the implement actions and procedures to minimize them, and possibly transform them into opportunities. Risk management is primarily risk prevention, and the provision of appropriate resources to risk symptoms and risk effects. By risk symptoms, I mean the intuition and documentation of potential risks associated with all aspects of a business. By risk effects, I mean the consequences and possible consequences of risk taking as well as unpredictable events that affect the health or even the life of a business.

## Risks Management Plan

A risk management plan is a document that provides an assessment of potential risks related to the operation of a business as well as set of strategies, procedures, actions and resources to address them. Do not let yourself get trapped into the idea that you are a small business; you don't need a risk management plan. This is wrong! In fact, a small business may have a greater need for a risk management plan than a big corporation, because you have less access to resources.

## Risks Assessment

The firs step toward developing a risk management plan is to assess the risk climate of your small business. By risk climate, I mean anything that can potentially pose a risk for business operation, growth and expansion. Usually, the risks are associated with people, property, and liability.

*People-based risks:* I group in that category all risks related to the small business owner, the employees, the partners, and the clients. Current examples in that category include, but are not limited to
  • accident in the workplace or related to a work assignment,
  • slips, falls and other accidents,
  • Acts of violence

*Property-based risks:* I call property-based risks all risks associated with any business property. In this category we may find items such as fire, natural catastrophe, crime and vandalism, and other similar risks.

*Liability-based risks:* Liability-based risks include all risks that are related to the legal operation and employment practices of the business. That category encompasses items like
  • Contracts,

- Copyright law violations
- Defamation,
- Employment discrimination,
- Harassments,
- Negligence,
- Premises liability,
- Securities law violations
- And other common liabilities.

I would advise a small business manager or owner to brainstorm all possible risks in writing. From the list, you can request the service of a professional to make a thorough and systematic risk assessment. You can ask your consultant to help you categorize the risks in terms of high, moderate, and low severity and frequency. Here is a matrix, which will probably be helpful to you when conducting your risks assessment.

**Figure 26**

**Risk Frequency and Severity Analysis Matrix**

| Frequency | Severity | | |
|---|---|---|---|
| | High | Moderate | **Low** |
| High | | | |
| Moderate | | | |
| **Low** | | | |

Based on the internal and external environments of your business, you will define what high, moderate, and low frequency mean; you will indicate what high, moderate, and low severity mean. Their definition will be different from one business to another. It is not always easy to determine the level of frequency and severity of risks, partly because the information may not be available. However, your consultant can use risk quantification formulae, which can provide you relatively good information to make your decisions.

## Risks Treatment Options

Some risk analysis formulae can provide you information in financial terms, so you can decide which risks treatment option (s) will work best for you. Risk treatment options mean simply the possible choices of decision that you have in terms of how you plan to address the risks that you identified. The most common options are:

- Risk avoidance,
- Risk reduction,
- Risk retention,
- Risk sharing,
- And risk transference.

*Risk avoidance:* Risk avoidance refers to the fact that some risks have high levels of frequency and severity, and are not worth taken. Therefore, you may decide to adopt procedures that prohibit any activity that can lead to such identified risks. You may for example decide not to sell a particular product or offer a specific service because of the associated liability. You can avoid undertaking any activity that you think is too costly for your business.

*Risk reduction:* A risk may carry a high or moderate level of frequency and a low level of severity. As a risk taker, you decide to deal with it, to the extent that you will take some actions or measure to reduce the occurrence. This is called risk reduction. For example, you may decide to sell a product with high incidence of shoplifting, and put it in a locked transparent shelf that only your store employees can access. You may avoid having a certain amount of cash in the counter, using locked cash boxes, using secured window for payment during certain hours, or make daily cash deposits.

*Risk retention:* If the occurrence and the severity of a risk are low, you may decide to live with it, and pay for the loss whenever it occurs. This option is called risk retention. In fact, any risk related to your business that you cannot do anything to influence is a retention risk by default. Most of the time, you deal with the consequences in the aftermath of an occurrence.

*Risk sharing:* There may be instances when you can partner with another company or provider to do business while there are some risks involved. Instead of refusing the deal, you may want to share the costs related to the risks with your partner or provider. This practice is known as risk sharing.

*Risk transference:* Risk transfer means simply that you transfer to another party the costs associated to the risks of an activity or operation of your business. An insurance policy, an indemnity agreement, and a waiver are examples of risk transfer decisions.

## Risk Management Provision

Risk management provision is the set of actions, procedures, and tools that you put in place to prevent and manage risks and emergency situations. The best way to manage risks is by practicing prevention.

When an entrepreneur starts a business, the risk is for the individual and the business. In business, the best translation of risk is financial loss regardless of the type of risk. Some risks are avoidable. Some are not. Therefore, there needs to be provision to prevent some risks to happen, and manage these that are unavoidable when they occurred. This is the purpose of a risk management system. Obviously, a risk management system is based on the information collected from the business risk assessment. An effective risk management system must include provision for people-based, property-based, and liability-based risks. The provisions will vary from one business to another, given the fact that every business is a relatively unique case.

*People-based risk provisions:* People based risk provisions concern prevention strategies and insurance plans related to all internal (business owners and employees) and external stakeholders (business partners, providers, clients or customers) of your business. These provisions include, but are not limited to:
- Safeguarding any activity that carries risks and hazards,
- Establishing procedures for maintenance and safe utilization of vehicles, machines, and equipment,
- Inspection of non-company owned vehicles (registration, insurance, etc),

- Establishing standards of qualifications for drivers and users of machines and equipment,
- Making prompt reparation or change where there is risk for slips, falls, or other accidents,
- Organizing safety training for employees,
- Ensuring that first aid kit, guidelines for personal protective equipment are readily available on site,
- Introducing policies about assaults, physical fights, and harassments;
- Obtaining formal guarantees from providers or suppliers that the products you are selling will not do harm if used properly.

*Property-based risks provisions:* Property-based risk provisions include all preventive measures and procedures and insurance plans concerning all property owned by the business. These provisions include, but are not limited to:

- Fire prevention (smoke detector, extinguisher, and inspection),
- Maintenance of storage, electrical equipment, gas appliance, and heating equipment,
- Proper storage of flammable liquids,
- Proper insurance and equipment insurance warranty,
- Burglary prevention through control of access to property buildings and a surveillance system,
- Robbery prevention,
- Vandalism prevention,
- Computer crime prevention.

*Liability-based risks provision:* Liability-based risk provision package insurance coverage for all potential liability claims that can affect the operation or even existence of the business. These provisions include, but are not limited to:

- Liability insurance
- Tort liability,
- Contract liability,
- Worker's compensation,
- Business interruption insurance,
- And all other legally required and appropriate insurance plans for your business.

## DO IT YOURSELF!

1. What are the potential risks associated with your business?

2. Which risk management treatment option do you like the most? Why?

3. Identify some basic risk management decisions that you would make mandatory for your business!

# Bibliography

Allison, M. and Kaye, J.(1997). *Strategic Planning for Nonprofit Organizations. A Practical Guide and Workbook.* New York: John Willey &Sons.

Bateman, T.S. and Snell, S.(1999). *Management. Building competitive advantage.* 4th. Edition. Boston: Irwin/McGraw-Hill.

Berle, G. and Kirschner, P.(1996). *The International Instant Business Plan.* California: Puma Publishing Company.

Bittel, L. L. and Newstrom, J. W. (1990). What every supervisor should know, 6th edition. NY: McGraw-Hill.

Buckingham, M. and Clifton, D. O. (2001). *Now, Discover your strengths.* NY: The Free Press.

Buckingham, M. and Coffman, C. (1999). *First, Break all the rules.* NY: Simon & Schuster.

Burnett, C. (1986). *One more time.* NY: Random House.

Collins, J.(2001). *Good to Great.* NY: Harper Collins.

Covello, J. and Hazelgren, B. (1998). *Your first business plan.* 3rd. edition. Naperville: Sourcebooks.

Diamond, M.R. and Williams, J.L. (1996). *How to incorporate.* 3rd. edition. NY: John Wiley & Sons.

Dollinger, M.J. (1999). *Entrepreneurship. Strategies and Resources.* 2nd. Edition. New Jersey: Prentice Hall.

Ferrell, O. C. and Fraedrich, J. (1994). *Business Ethics. Ethical decision making and cases.* 2nd. Edition. Boston: Houghton Mifflin Company.

Hill, C.W.L. and Jones, G.R. (1995). *Strategic Management. An integrated approach.* 3rd. edition. Boston: Houghton Mifflin Company.

Jean-Francois, E. (2005). *Negotiational leadership and influence strategies.* Tampa: Springfield College.

Lewis, J. P. (1995). *Fundamentals of Project Management.* NY: Amacom.

Mandela, N.(1994). *The long walk to freedom.* NY: Little Brown and Co.

McCarthy, K.W.(1992). *The on-purpose person. Making your life make sense.* Winter Park: US Partners Inc.

Morrisey, G.L. (1986). *Management by objectives and results in the public sector.* Massachussetts: Addison-Wesley Publishing company.

Susan M.(1996). *Understanding Business.* Chicago: Irwin.

O'Neil, William J.(2004). *The successful investor.* NY: McGraw-Hill.

Plunkett, W.R.; Attner, R.F.; and Allen,G.S. (2002). *Management. Meeting and exceeding customer expectations.* Mason: Thomson Learning.

Schneeman, A.(1997). *The Law of corporations, partnerships, and sole proprietorships.* 2nd Edition. Albany: Delmar Publisher.

Spiro, H.T.(1988). *Finance for the nonfinancial manager.* 3rd edition. NY: John Wiley and Sons.

Townsend,P.L. and Gebhardt,J. E.(1990). *Commit to Quality.* NY: John
Wiley & Sons.

Tway, P.(1993). *Success Common Sense and the Small business.* Cincinnati:
Betterway Books.

Wilson,S.B.(1994). *Goal setting.* NY: Amacom.

Yate, M.(1994). *Hiring the best.* 4th Edition. Massachussetts: Adams
Media Corporation.

# Appendices

# Glossary of Terms

**Accounts payable**
Trade accounts of businesses representing obligations to pay for goods and services received.

**Accounts receivable**
Trade accounts of businesses representing moneys due for goods sold or services rendered evidenced by notes, statements, invoices, or other written evidence of a present obligation.

**Accounting**
The recording, classifying, summarizing, and interpreting in a significant manner and in terms of money, transactions, and events of a financial character.

**Accrual**
Method of accounting in which you match revenue with expense regardless of when the cash may or may not be collected.

**Annual Budget**
For an existing business, this is a realistic budget for the current fiscal year based on past income and expenditures. It includes anticipated changes in income and spending that may occur during the year. For a start-up business, this is a realistic projection of the income and costs of doing business for a year.

**Audit**
Verification of financial records and accounting procedures generally conducted by a CPA or accounting firm.

**Balance sheet**
Financial statement showing assets and liabilities at a specific time.

**Bank Account Reconciliation**
Comparing and matching your checkbook balance with your bank balance.

**Bankruptcy**
Based on the National bankruptcy Act, a business that cannot meet its debt obligations may file bankruptcy by petitioning a federal district court for either reorganization of its debts or liquidation of its assets.

**Breakeven point**
The breakeven point is that point at which the volume of sales or revenues exactly equals total expenses.

**Business plan**
A document that describes the goals and objectives of an existing or proposed business as well as the action plan and strategies to achieve them.

**Bond**
A third party obligation promising to pay if a vendor does not fulfill its valid obligations under a contract.

**Canceled loan**
The annulment or rescission of an approved loan prior to disbursement.

**Capital asset**
An asset that is purchased for long-term use such as machinery and equipment.

**Capital expenditures**
Business spending on additional plant equipment and inventory.

**Cash Flow Projections**
A month-by-month future projection of income and expenditures over a period of time, usually a year. The projections for an existing business are based on current cash flow patterns. Cash flows can be calculated for any given period of time, normally done on a monthly basis.

**Closing**
Actions and procedures required to affect the documentation and disbursement of loan funds after the application has been approved

and the execution of all required documentation and its filing and recording where required.

**Closed loan**
Any loan for which funds have been disbursed and all required documentation has been executed, received, and reviewed.

**Collateral**
Something of value - securities, evidence of deposit, or other property - pledged to support the repayment of an obligation.

**Collateral document**
A legal document covering the item(s) pledged as collateral on a loan, i.e., note, mortgages, assignment.

**Consortium**
A coalition of organizations, such as banks and corporations, set up to fund ventures requiring large capital resources.

**Corporation**
A group of persons granted a state charter legally recognizing them as a separate entity having its own rights, privileges, and liabilities distinct from those of its members. Usually, the process of incorporating is completed with the state's secretary of state.

**Costs**
Money obligated for goods and services received during a given period of time, regardless of when ordered or whether paid for.

**Credit report**
A listing of an individual or company's history of repaying past loans and other liabilities.

**Credit rating**
A grade assigned to a business concern to denote the net worth and credit standing to which the concern is entitled in the opinion of the rating agency as a result of its investigation.

**Debenture**
Debt instrument evidencing the holder's right to receive interest and principal installments from the named obligor. Applies to all forms of unsecured, long-term debt evidenced by a certificate of debt.

**Debt capital**
Business financing that normally requires periodic interest payments and repayment of the principal within a specified time.

**Debt financing**
The provision of long term loans to small business concerns in exchange for debt securities or a note.

**Deed of trust**
A document under seal which, when delivered, transfers a present interest in property. May be held as collateral.

**Defaults**
The nonpayment of principal and/or interest on the due date as provided by the terms and conditions of the note.

**Deferred loan**
Loans whose principal and or interest installments are postponed for a specified period of time.

**Depreciation**
Decrease in the value of equipment over time. Depreciation of equipment used for business is a tax-deductible expense.

**Disbursement**
The actual payout to borrower of loan funds, in whole or part. It may be concurrent with the closing or follow it.

**DUNS**
**Data Universal Numbering System (DUNS) is a** database maintained by Dun and Bradstreet that is used by the Government to identify each contractor and their location(s). This number is required to register with the Central Contractor Register (CCR) that is used by the government's

electronic commerce/electronic data interchange (EC/EDI) system called FACNET.

**Earning power**
Demonstrated ability of a business to earn a profit, over time, while following good accounting practices.

**Employer identification number (EIN)**
A number obtained by a business from the IRS by filing form SS-4. The EIN represents what the Social Security Number is for an individual. It is required to open a bank account for a business.

**Employment Eligibility Verification, I-9.**
Form that employers are required to have all employees complete as proof of eligibility to work in the U.S.

**Employment Taxes**
Taxes that employers are required to withhold from employee wages, including:
- Federal Income Tax
- Social Security and Medicare Taxes (FICA)
- Federal Unemployment (FUTA) Taxes.

**Enterprise**
Aggregation of all establishments owned by a parent company. An enterprise can consist of a single, independent establishment or it can include subsidiaries or other branch establishments under the same ownership and control.

**Entrepreneur**
One who assumes the financial risk of the initiation, operation, and management of a given business or undertaking.

**Equity**
An ownership interest in a business.

**Equity financing**
The provision of funds for capital or operating expenses in exchange

for capital stock, stock purchase warrants, and options in the business financed without any guaranteed return, but with the opportunity to share in the company's profits.

### Equity partnership
A limited partnership arrangement for providing startup and seed capital to businesses.

### Escrow accounts
Funds placed in trust with a third party by a borrower for a specific purpose and to be delivered to the borrower only upon the fulfillment of certain conditions.

**Federal Deposit Insurance Corporation (FDIC)** is a United States government corporation created by the Glass-Steagall Act of 1933, which provides deposit insurance guarantees for checking and savings accounts of bank members, up to $250,000 per depositor per bank.

### Federal tax deposit coupon
Coupons automatically sent by the IRS about six weeks after a business applies for an Employer Identification Number (EIN). They are used for depositing employment taxes. Each coupon shows the deposit amount, the type of tax, the period for which the deposit is made and your phone number. You will not use it if you don't have employees.

### Federal Insurance Contributions Act (FICA)
Tax imposed by the federal government on both employees and employers to fund Social Security and Medicare. A portion of the tax is withheld from employee earnings and remitted to the IRS. Employers also contribute a portion of the tax.

### Federal Unemployment Tax (FUTA)
Tax that federal and state employers pay to cover unemployment compensation for workers who lose their jobs. No funds are withheld from an employee's pay. Payments are made using IRS Form 940 or 940-EZ, Employer's Annual Federal Unemployment (FUTA) Tax Return.

**Financial reports**
Reports commonly required from applicants request for financial assistance, e.g.:
Balance Sheet - A report of the status of a firm's assets, liabilities and owner's equity at a given time.
Income Statement - A report of revenue and expense which shows the results of business operations or net income for a specified period of time.

**Financing**
New funds provided to a business, by either loans, purchase of debt securities, or capital stock.

**Fiscal year**
Any 12-month period used by a company or government as an accounting period.

**Flow chart**
A graphical representation for the definition, analysis, or solution of a problem, in which symbols are used to represent operations, data, flow, equipment, etc.

**Foreclosure**
The act by the mortgagee or trustee upon default in the payment of interest or principal of a mortgage of enforcing payment of the debt by selling the underlying security.

**Franchising**
A continuing relationship in which the franchisor provides a licensed privilege to the franchisee to do business and offers assistance in organizing, training, merchandising, marketing, and managing in return for a consideration. Franchising is a form of business by which the owner (franchisor) of a product, service, or method obtains distribution through affiliated dealers (franchisees). The product, method, or service being marketed is usually identified by the franchisor's brand name, and the holder of the privilege (franchisee) is often given exclusive access to a defined geographical area.

## Gross Domestic Product (GDP)
The most comprehensive single measure of aggregate economic output. Represents the market value of the total output of the goods and services produced by a nation's economy.

## Gross National Product (GNP)
A measure of a nation's aggregate economic output. Since 1991 GDP, a slightly different calculation, has replaced GNP as a measure of U.S. economic output.

## Guaranteed loan
A loan made and serviced by a lending institution under agreement that a governmental agency will purchase the guaranteed portion if the borrower defaults.

## Innovation
Introduction of a new idea into the marketplace in the form of a new product or service or an improvement in organization or process.

## Insolvency
The inability of a borrower to meet financial obligations as they mature or having insufficient assets to pay legal debts.

## Interest
An amount paid a lender for the use of funds.

## Inverse order of maturity
When payments are received from borrowers that are larger than the authorized repayment schedules, the overpayment is credited to the final installments of the principal, which reduces the maturity of the loan and does not affect the original repayment schedule.

## IRA or 401(k)
Individual Retirement Accounts

## Lease
A contract between the owner (leassor) and the tenant (leassee) stating the conditions under which the tenant may occupy or use the property.

**Legal rate of interest**
The maximum rate of interest fixed by the laws of the various states which a lender may charge a borrower for the use of money.

**Lending institution**
Any institution, including a commercial bank, savings and loan association, commercial finance company, or other lender qualified to participate with SBA in the making of loans.

**Litigation**
Refers to a loan in "liquidation status" which has been referred to attorneys for legal action.

**Loan agreement**
Agreement to be executed by borrower, containing pertinent terms, conditions, covenants, and restrictions.

**Loan payoff amount**
The total amount of money needed to meet a borrower's obligation on a loan.

**Merger**
A combination of two or more corporations wherein the dominant unit absorbs the passive ones, the former continuing operation usually under the same name.

**National Standard Employer Identification Number**
This is a number used to electronically transmit health insurance claims.

**Negotiation**
The face to face process used by two parties or more to reach agreement.

**Net worth**
Property owned (assets), minus debts and obligations owed (liabilities).

## Notes and accounts receivable
A secured or unsecured receivable evidenced by a note or open account arising from activities involving liquidation and disposal of loan collateral.

## Obligations
Technically defined as "amount of orders placed, contracts awarded, services received, and similar transactions during a given period which will require payments during the same or a future period."

## Ordinary interest
Simple interest based on a year of 360 days, contrasting with exact interest having a base year of 365 days.

## Outlays
Net disbursements (cash payments in excess of cash receipts) for administrative expenses and for loans and related costs and expenses (e.g., gross disbursements for loans and expenses minus loan repayments, interest and fee income collected, and reimbursements received for services performed for other agencies).

## Outsourcing
The practice of using subcontractors rather than paid employees.

## Partnership
A legal relationship existing between two or more persons contractually associated as joint principals in a business.

## Patent
Grant of a property right to an inventor, issued by the Patent and Trademark Office. A new patent is issued for 20 years from the date on which the application for the patent was filed in the United States or, in special cases, from the date an earlier related application was filed, subject to the payment of maintenance fees.

## Power of attorney
An agreement authorizing someone (generally an attorney) to act as

your agent. This agreement may be general (complete authority) or special (limited authority).

**Prime rate**
Interest rate which is charged to business borrowers having the highest credit ratings for short term borrowing.

**Product liability**
Type of tort or civil liability that applies to product manufacturers and sellers.

**Professional and trade associations**
Non-profit, cooperative, and voluntary organizations that are designed to help their members in dealing with problems of mutual interest.

**Return on investment**
The amount of profit (return) based on the amount of resources (funds) used to produce it. Also the ability of a given investment to earn a return for its use.

**SBA**
The U. S. Small Business Administration.

**SBDC**
Small Business Development Centers are university-based center for the delivery of joint government, academic, and private sector services for the benefit of small business and the national welfare. They are located throughout the United States and are administered by the SBA.

**SBIC**
**Small Business Investment Corporation that** are licensed by the SBA as federally funded private venture capital firms. Money is available to small businesses under a variety of agreements.

**SCORE**
The Service Corps of Retired Executives is a volunteer management assistance program of the SBA. The SCORE provide one-on-one counseling and workshops and seminars for small businesses.

**Secondary market**
Those who purchase an interest in a loan from an original lender, such as banks, institutional investors, insurance companies, credit unions, and pension funds.

**SIC**
**Standard Industrial Classification Code is a** four-digit number assigned to identify a business based on the type of business or trade involved. SIC numbers are usually published in a directory by the Department of Commerce.

**Simple interest**
Interest paid only on the principal of a loan.

**Sole proprietorship**
Form of business owned by one individual personally liable for all debts of the business to the full extent of his or her property. The owner has full control over the business.

**Turnover** (Business)
Turnover is the number of times that an average inventory of goods is sold during a fiscal year or some designated period. Care must be taken to ensure that the average inventory and net sales are both reduced to the same denominator; that is, divide inventory at cost into sales at cost or divide inventory at selling price into sales at selling price. Do not mix cost price with selling price. The turnover, when accurately computed, is one measure of the efficiency of a business.

**Undelivered orders**
The amount of orders for goods and services outstanding for which the liability has not yet accrued. For practical purposes, represents obligations incurred for which goods have not been delivered or services not performed.

**Unfair labor practice**
Action by either the employer or union which violates the provisions of EO 11491 as amended.

**Usury**

Interest which exceeds the legal rate charged to a borrower for the use of money.

**Venture capital**

Money used to support new or unusual commercial undertakings; equity, risk, or speculative capital. This funding is provided to new or existing firms that exhibit above-average growth rates, a significant potential for market expansion, and the need for additional financing for business maintenance or expansion.

**Workers' compensation**

A state-mandated form of insurance covering workers injured in job-related accidents. In some states the state is the insurer; in other states insurance must be acquired from commercial insurance firms. Insurance rates are based on a number of factors, including salaries, firm history, and risk of occupation.

# Sample Bylaws: Bylaws of Rainbow Printing, Inc.

(Adapted from several corporation Bylaws)

Article I – Offices

The principal office of the Corporation in the State of Georgia shall be located in Atlanta. The Corporation may have such other offices, either within or without the State of Georgia, as the Board of Directors may designate or as the business of the Corporation may require from time to time.

Article II – Shareholders

Section 1. Annual Meeting. The annual meeting of the shareholders shall be held on the 2nd day in the month of June in each year, beginning with the year 200x, at the hour of 2:00 Pm, for the purpose of electing Directors and for the transaction of such other business as may come before the meeting. If the day fixed for the annual meeting shall be a legal holiday in the State of Florida, such meeting shall be held on the next succeeding business day. If the election of Directors shall not be held on the day designated herein for any annual meeting of the shareholders, or at any adjournment thereof, the Board of Directors shall cause the election to be held at a special meeting of the shareholders as soon thereafter as conveniently may be.

Section 2. Special Meeting. Special meetings of the shareholders, for any purpose or purposes, unless otherwise prescribed by statute, may be called by the President or by the Board of Directors, and shall be called by the President at the request of the holders of not less than sixty percent (60%) of all the outstanding shares of the Corporation entitled to vote at the meeting.

Section 3. Place of Meeting. The Board of Directors may designate any place, either within or without the State of Florida, unless otherwise prescribed by statute, as the place of meeting for any annual meeting or for any special meeting. A waiver of notice signed by all shareholders entitled to vote at a meeting may designate any place, either within or without the State of Georgia, unless otherwise prescribed by statute, as the place for holding such meeting. If no designation is made, the place of meeting shall be the principal office of the Corporation.

Section 4. Notice of Meeting. Written notice stating the place, day and hour of the meeting and, in case of a special meeting, the purpose or purposes for which the meeting is called, shall unless otherwise prescribed by statute, be before the date of the meeting, to each shareholder of record entitled to vote at such meeting. If mailed, such notice shall be deemed to be delivered when deposited in the United States Mail, addressed to the shareholders at his address as it appears on the stock transfer books of the Corporation, with postage thereon paid.

Section 5. Closing of Transfer Books or Fixing of record. For the purpose of determining shareholders entitled to notice of or to vote at any meeting of shareholders or any adjournment thereof, or shareholders entitled to receive payment of any dividend, or in order to make a determination of shareholders for any other to make a determination of shareholders for any other proper purpose, the Board of Directors of the Corporation may provide that the stock transfer books shall be closed for a stated period, but not to exceed in any case sixty (6) days. If the stock transfer books shall be closed for the purpose of determining shareholders entitled to notice of or to vote at a meeting of shareholders, such books shall be closed for at least (5) five days immediately preceding such meeting. In lieu of closing the stock transfer books, the Board of Directors may fix in advance a date as the record date for any such determination of shareholders, such date in any case to be not more than thirty days and, in any case of a meeting of shareholders, not less than five (5) days, prior to the date on which the particular action requiring such determination of shareholders is to be taken. If the stock transfer books are not closed and no record date is fixed for the determination of shareholders, or shareholders entitled to receive payment of a dividend, the date on which the resolution of the Board of Directors declaring such dividend is adopted, as the case may be, shall be the record date for such determination of shareholders. When a determination of shareholders entitled to vote at any meeting of shareholders has been made as provided in this section, such determination shall apply to any adjournment thereof.

Section 6. Voting Lists. The officer or agent having charge of the stock transfer books for shares of the corporation shall make a complete list of the shareholders entitled to vote at each meeting of shareholders or any adjournment thereof, arranged in alphabetical order, with the address of and the number of shares held by each. Such list shall be produced and kept open at the time and place of the meeting and shall be subject to the inspection of any shareholder during the whole time of the meeting for the purposes thereof.

Section 7. Quorum. A majority of the outstanding shares of the corporation entitled to vote, represented in person or by proxy, shall constitute a quorum at a meeting of shareholders. If less than a majority of the outstanding shares are represented at a meeting, a majority of the shares so represented may adjourn the meeting from time to time without further notice. At such adjourned meeting at which a quorum shall be present or represented, any business may be transacted which might have been transacted at the meeting as originally noticed. The shareholders present at a duly organized meeting may continue to transact business until adjournment, notwithstanding the withdrawal of enough shareholders to leave less than a quorum.

Section 8. Proxies. At all meetings of shareholders, a shareholder may vote in person or by proxy executed in writing by the shareholder or by his or her duly authorized attorney-in-fact. Such proxy shall be filled with the secretary of the Corporation before or at the time of the meeting. A meeting of the Board of Directors may be held by means of a telephone conference or similar communication equipment by which all persons participating in the meeting can hear each other, and participation in a meeting under such circumstances shall constitute presence at the meeting.

Section 9. Voting of Shares. Each outstanding share entitled to vote shall be entitled to one vote upon each matter submitted to a vote at a meeting of shareholders.

Section 10. Voting of Shares by Certain Holders. Shares standing in the name of another corporation may be voted by such officer, agent or proxy as the Bylaws of such corporation may prescribe or, in the absence of such provision, as the Board of Directors of such corporation may determine.

Shares held by an administrator, executor, guardian or conservator may be voted by him either in person or by proxy, without a transfer of such shares into his name. Shares standing in the name of a trustee may be voted by him, either in person or by proxy, but no trustee shall be entitled to vote shares held by him without a transfer of such shares into his name.

Shares standing in the name of a receiver may be voted by such receiver, and shares held by or under the control of a receiver may be voted by such receiver without the transfer thereof into his name, if authority to do so be contained in an appropriate order of the court by which such receiver was appointed.

A shareholder whose shares are pledged shall be entitled to vote such shares until the shares have been transferred into the name of the pledge, and thereafter the pledge shall be entitled to vote the shares so transferred.

Shares of its own stock belonging to the Corporation shall not be voted directly or indirectly, at any meeting, and shall not be counted in determining the total number of outstanding shares at any given time.

Section 11. Informal Action by Shareholders. Unless otherwise provided by law, any action required to be taken at a meeting of the shareholders, or any other action which may be taken at a meeting of the shareholders, may be taken without a meeting if a consent in writing, setting forth the action so taken, shall be signed by all of the shareholders entitled to vote with respect to the subject matter thereof.

Article III – Board of Directors

Section 1. General Powers. The business and affairs of the Corporation shall be managed by its Board of Directors.

Section 2. Number, Tenure and Qualifications. The number of directors of the Corporation shall be fixed by the Board of Directors, but in no event shall be less than one (1). Each director shall hold office until the next annual meeting of shareholders and until his successor shall have been elected and qualified.

Section 3. Regular Meeting. A regular meeting of the Board of Directors shall be held without other notice than this Bylaw immediately after, and at the same place as, the annual meeting of shareholders. The Board of Directors may provide, by resolution, the time and place for the holding of additional regular meeting without notice other than such resolution.

Section 4. Special Meetings. Special meetings of the Board of Directors may be called by or at the request of the President or any two directors. The person or persons authorized to call special meetings of the Board of Directors may fix the place for holding any special meeting of the Board of Directors called by them.

Section 5. Notice. Notice of any special meeting shall be given at least one (1) day previous thereto by written notice delivered personally or mailed to each director at his business address, or by telegram. If mailed, such notice shall be deemed to be delivered when deposited in the United States Mail so addressed, with postage thereon paid. If notice be given by telegram, such notice shall be deemed to be delivered when the telegram is delivered to the telegraph company. Any directors may waive notice of any meeting. The attendance of a director at a meeting shall constitute a waiver of notice of such meeting, except where a director attends a meeting for the express purpose of objecting to the transaction of any business because the meeting is not lawfully called or convened.

Section 6. Quorum. A majority of the number of directors fixed by section 2 of this article III constitute a quorum for the transaction of business at any meeting of the Board of Directors, but if less than such majority is present at a meeting, a majority of the directors present may adjourn the meeting from time to time without further notice.

Section 7. Action Without Meeting. Any action that may be taken by the Board of Directors at a meeting may be taken without a meeting if a consent in writing, setting forth the action so to be taken, shall be signed before such action by all of the directors.

Section 9. Vacancies. Any vacancy occurring in the Board of Directors may be filled by the affirmative vote of a majority of the remaining directors though less than a quorum of the Board of Directors, unless otherwise provided by law. A director elected to fill a vacancy shall be elected for the unexpired term of his predecessor in office. Any directorship to be filled by reason of an increase in the number of directors may be filled by election by the Board of Directors for a term of office continuing only until the next election of directors by the shareholders.

Section 10. Compensation. By resolution of the Board of Directors, each director may be paid his expenses, if any, of attendance at each meeting of the Board of Directors, and may be paid a stated salary as a director or a fixed sum for attendance at each meeting of the Board of Directors or both. No such payment shall preclude any director from serving the Corporation in any other capacity and receiving compensation therefore.

Section 11. Presumption of Assent. A director of the Corporation who is present at a meeting of the Board of Directors at which action on any corporate matter is taken shall be presumed to have assented to the action taken unless his dissent shall be entered in the minutes of the meeting or unless he shall file his written dissent to such action with the person acting as the Secretary of the meeting before the adjournment thereof, or shall forward such dissent by registered mail to the Secretary of the Corporation immediately after the adjournment of the meeting. Such right to dissent shall not apply to a director who voted in favor of such action.

Article IV – Officers

Section 1. Number. The officers of the Corporation shall be a President, one or more Vice Presidents, a secretary and a Treasurer, each of whom shall be elected by the Board of Directors. Such other officers and assistant officers as may be deemed necessary may be elected or appointed by the Board of Directors, including a Chairman of the Board. In its discretion, the Board of Directors may leave unfilled for any such period as it may determine any office except those of President and Secretary. Any two or more offices may be held by the same person, except for the offices of President and Secretary which may not be held by the same person. Officers may be directors or shareholders of the Corporation.

Section 2. Election and Term of Office. The officers of the Corporation to be elected by the Board of Directors shall be elected annually by the Board of Directors at the first meeting of the Board of Directors held each annual meeting of the shareholders. If the election of officers shall not be held at such meeting, such election shall be held as soon thereafter as conveniently may be. Each officer shall hold office until his successor shall have been duly elected and shall have qualified, or until his death, or until he shall resign or shall have been removed in the manner hereinafter provided.

Section 3. Removal. Any officer or agent may be removed by the Board of Directors whenever, in its judgment, the best interests of the Corporation will be served thereby, but such removal shall be without prejudice to the contract rights, if any, of the person so removed. Election of appointment of an officer or agent shall not of itself create contract rights, and such appointment shall be terminable at will.

Section 4. Vacancies. A vacancy in any office because of death, resignation, removal, disqualification, or otherwise, may be filled by the Board of Directors for the unexpired portion of the term.

Section 5. President. The President shall be the principal executive officer of the Corporation and, subject to the control of the Board of Directors, shall in general supervise and control all of the business and affairs of the Corporation. He shall, when present, preside at all meetings of the shareholders and of the Board of Directors, unless there is a Chairman of the Board, in which case the Chairman shall preside.

He may sign, with the Secretary or any other proper officer of the Corporation thereunto authorized by the Board of directors, certificates for shares of the Corporation, any deeds, mortgages, bonds, contracts, or other instruments which the Board of Directors has authorized to be executed, except in cases where the signing and execution thereof shall be expressly delegated by the Board of Directors or by these Bylaws to some other officer or agent of the Corporation, or shall be required by law to be otherwise signed or executed; and in general shall perform all duties incident to the office of the President and such other duties as may be prescribed by the Board of Directors from time to time.

Section 6. Vice President. In the absence of the president or in event of his death, inability or refusal to act, the Vice President shall perform the duties of the President, and when so acting, shall have all the powers of and be subject to all the restrictions upon the President. The Vice President shall perform such other duties as from time to time may be assigned to him/her by the President in order of rank as determined by the Board of Directors. If no such rank has been determined, then each Vice President shall succeed to the duties of the President in order of date of election, the earliest date having the first rank.

Section 7. Secretary. The Secretary shall: (a) keep the minutes of the proceedings of the shareholders and the Board of Directors in one or more minute books provided for that purpose; (b) see that all notices are duly given in accordance with the provisions of these Bylaws or as required by law; (c) be custodian of the corporate records and of the seal of the Corporation and see that the seal of the Corporation is affixed to all documents, the execution of which on behalf of the Corporation under its seal is duly authorized; (d) keep a register of the post office address of each shareholder which shall be furnished to the Secretary by such shareholders; (e) sign with the President certificates for shares of the Corporation, the issuance of which shall have been authorized by resolution of the Board of Directors; (f) have general charge of the stock transfer books of the Corporation; and (g) in general perform all duties incident to the office of the Secretary and such other duties as from time to time may be assigned to him/her by the President or by the Board of Directors.

Section 8. Treasure. The Treasurer shall: (a) have charge and custody of and be responsible for all funds and securities of the Corporation; (b) receive and give receipts for moneys due and payable to the Corporation from any source whatsoever, and deposit all such moneys in the name of the Corporation in such banks, trust companies or other depositories as shall be selected in accordance with the provisions of Article VI of these Bylaws; and (c) in general perform all of the duties incident to the office of Treasurer and such duties as from time to time may be assigned to him/her by the President or by the Board of Directors. If required by the Board of Directors, the Treasurer shall give a bond for the faithful discharge of his duties in such sum and with such sureties as the Board of Directors shall determine.

Section 9. Salaries. The salaries of the officers shall be fixed from time to time by the Board of Directors, and no officer shall be prevented from receiving such salary by reason of the fact that he/she is also a director of the Corporation.

Article V – Indemnity

The Corporation shall indemnify its directors, officers and employees as follows:

(a)   Every director, officer, or employee of the Corporation shall be indemnified by the Corporation against all expenses and liabilities, including counsel fees, reasonably incurred by or imposed upon him in connection with any proceeding to which he may become involved, by reason of his being or having been a director, officer, employee or agent of the Corporation as a director, officer, employee or agent of the Corporation or is or was serving at the request of the Corporation as a director, officer, employee or agent of the corporation, partnership, joint venture, trust or enterprise, or any settlement thereof, whether or not he is a director, officer, employee or agent at the time such expenses are incurred, except in such cases wherein the director, officer, or employee is adjudged guilty of willful misfeasance or malfeasance in the performance of his duties; provided that in the event of a settlement the indemnification herein shall apply only when the Board of Directors approves such settlement and reimbursement as being for the best interests of the Corporation.

(b) The Corporation shall provide to any person who is or was a director, officer, employee, or agent of the Corporation or is or was serving at the request of the Corporation as a director, officer, employee or agent of the corporation, partnership, joint venture, trust or enterprise, the indemnity against expenses of suit, litigation or other proceedings which is specifically permissible under applicable law.

(c) The Board of Directors may, in its discretion, direct the purchase of liability insurance by way of implementing the provisions of this Article V.

Article VI – Contracts – Loans – Checks and Deposits

Section 1. Contracts. The Board of Directors may authorize any officers, agents or agents, to enter into any contract or execute and deliver any instrument in the name of and on behalf of the Corporation, and such authority may be general or confined to specific instances.

Section 2. Loans. No loans shall be contracted on behalf of the Corporation and no evidences of indebtedness shall be issued in its name unless authorized by a resolution of the Board of Directors. Such authority may be general or confined to specific instances.

Section 3. Checks, Drafts. All checks, drafts or other orders for payment of money, notes or other evidences of indebtedness issued in the name of the Corporation, shall be signed by such officer or officers, agent or agents of the Corporation and in such manner as shall from time to time be determined by resolution of the Board of Directors.

Section 4. Deposits. All funds of the Corporation not otherwise employed shall be deposited from time to time to the credit of the Corporation in such banks, trust companies or other depositories as the Board of Directors may select.

Article VII – Certificates for Shares and their Transfer

Section 1. Certificates for Shares. Certificates representing shares of the Corporation shall be in such form as shall be determined by the Board of Directors. Such certificates shall be signed by the President and by the Secretary or by such other officers authorized by law and by the Board of Directors so to do, and sealed with the corporate seal. All certificates for shares shall be consecutively numbered or otherwise identified. The name and addressed of the person to whom the shares represented thereby are issued, with the number of shares and date of issue, shall be entered on the stock transfer books of the Corporation. All certificates surrendered to the Corporation for transfer shall be cancelled and no new certificate shall be issued until the former certificate for a like number of shares shall have been surrendered and cancelled, except that in case of a lost, destroyed or mutilated certificate a new one may be issued therefore upon such terms and indemnity to the Corporation as the Board of Directors may prescribe.

Section 2. Transfer of Shares. Transfer of shares of the Corporation shall be made only on the stock transfer books of the Corporation by the holder of record thereof or by his legal representative, who shall furnish proper evidence of authority to transfer, or by his attorney thereunto authorized by power of attorney duly executed and filed with the Secretary of the Corporation, and on surrender for cancellation of the certificate for such shares. The person in whose name shares stand on the books of the Corporation shall be deemed by the Corporation to be the owner thereof for all purposes. Provided, however, that upon any action undertaken by the shareholders to elect S Corporation status pursuant to Section 1362 of the Internal Revenue Code and upon any shareholders agreement thereto restricting the transfer of said shares so as to disqualify said S Corporation status, said restriction on transfer shall be made a part of the Bylaws so long as said agreement is in force and effect.

Article VIII. Fiscal Year

The fiscal year of the Corporation shall begin on the first day of January and end on the 31$^{st}$ day of December of each year.

Article IX. Dividends

The Board of Directors may from time to time declare, and the Corporation may pay, dividends on its outstanding shares in the manner and upon the terms and conditions provided by law and its Articles of Incorporation.

Article X. Corporate Seal

The Board of Directors shall provide a corporate seal which shall be circular in form and shall have inscribed thereon the name of the Corporation and the state of incorporation and the words, "Corporate Seal".

Article XI. Waiver of Notice

Unless otherwise provided by law, whenever any notice is required to be given to any shareholder or director of the Corporation under the provisions of these Bylaws or under the provisions of the Articles of Incorporation or under the provisions of the applicable Business Corporation Act, a waiver thereof in writing, signed by the person or persons entitled to such notice, whether before or after the time stated therein, shall be deemed equivalent to the giving of such notice.

Article XII. Amendments

These Bylaws may be altered, amend or repealed and new Bylaws may be adopted by the Board of Directors at any regular or special meeting of the Board of Directors.

The above Bylaws are certified to have been adopted by the Board of Directors of the Corporation on the 2nd day of March 1999.
Secretary

# Small Business Administration offices

URL: www.sba.gov.

## Region 1

U.S. Small Business Administration
10 Causeway St.
Boston, MA 02222-1093
Phone: (617)565-8415
Fax: (617)565-8420
Serves Connecticut, Maine,
Massachusetts, New Hampshire,
Rhode Island, and Vermont.

## Region 2

U.S. Small Business Administration
26 Federal Plaza, Ste. 3108
New York, NY 10278
Phone: (212)264-1450
Fax: (212)264-0038
Serves New Jersey, New York, Puerto
Rico, and the Virgin Islands.

## Region 3

Serves Delaware, the District of Columbia, Maryland, Pennsylvania,
Virginia, and West Virginia. For the nearest field office, visit the Small
Business Administration online at www.sba.gov.

## Region 4

U.S. Small Business Administration
233 Peachtree St. NE
Harris Tower 1800
Atlanta, GA 30303
Phone: (404)331-4999
Fax: (404)331-2354
Serves Alabama, Florida, Georgia,
Kentucky, Mississippi, North
Carolina, South Carolina, and Tennessee.

Region 5
U.S. Small Business Administration
500 W. Madison St., Ste. 1240
Chicago, IL 60661-2511
Phone: (312)353-5000
Fax: (312)353-3426
Serves Illinois, Indiana, Michigan,
Minnesota, Ohio, and Wisconsin.


Region 6
U.S. Small Business Administration
4300 Amon Carter Blvd.
Dallas/Fort Worth, TX 76155
Phone: (817)885-6581
Fax: (817)885-6588
Serves Arkansas, Louisiana, New
Mexico, Oklahoma, and Texas.


Region 7
U.S. Small Business Administration
323 W. 8th St., Ste. 307
Kansas City, MO 64105-1500
Phone: (816)374-6380
Fax: (816)374-6339
Serves Iowa, Kansas, Missouri, and Nebraska.


Region 8
U.S. Small Business Administration
721 19th St., Ste. 400
Denver, CO 80202
Phone: (303)844-0500
Fax: (303)844-0506
Serves Colorado, Montana, North
Dakota, South Dakota, Utah, and Wyoming.

Region 9
U.S. Small Business Administration
455 Market St., Ste. 2200
San Francisco, CA 94105
Phone: (415)744-2118
Fax: (415)744-2119
Serves American Samoa, Arizona, California, Guam, Hawaii, Nevada, and the Trust Territory of the Pacific Islands.

Region 10
U.S. Small Business Administration
1200 6th Ave., Ste. 1805
Seattle, WA 98101-1128
Phone: (206)553-5676
Fax: (206)553-2872
Serves Alaska, Idaho, Oregon, and Washington.

# Small Business Development Centers

Alabama SBDC
UNIVERSITY OF ALABAMA - Birmingham
1500 1st Avenue North, R118
Birmingham, AL 35203
Phone: 205-307-6510
Fax: 205-307-6511
E-Mail: williamc@uab.edu
Website: http://www.asbdc.org

Alaska SBDC
UNIVERSITY OF ALASKA - ANCHORAGE
430 West Seventh Avenue, Suite 110
Anchorage, AK 99501-3550
Phone: 907-274 -7232
Fax: 907-274-9524
E-Mail: anjad@uaa.alaska.edu
Website: http://www.aksbdc.org

American Samoa SBDC
AMERICAN SAMOA COMMUNITY COLLEGE
P.O. Box 2609
Pago, American Samoa 96799
Phone: 011-684-699-4830
Fax: 011-684-699-6132
E-Mail: htalex@worldet.att.net
Website: http://www.as-sbdc.org

Arizona SBDC
ARIZONA SMALL BUSINESS DEVELOPMENT CENTER
NETWORK
Maricopa County Community College
2411 West 14th Street, Suite 114
Tempe, AZ 85281
Phone: (480)731-8722
Fax: (480)731-8729
E-Mail: janice.washington@domail.maricopa.edu
Website: https://www.azsbdc.net/Default.aspx

Arkansas SBDC
UNIVERSITY OF ARKANSAS at Little Rock
2801 South University Avenue, Rm 260
Little Rock, AR 72204
Phone: 501-683-7700
Fax: 501-683-7720
E-Mail: jmroderick@ualr.edu
Website: http://asbdc.ualr.edu

California - Santa Ana SBDC
Tri-County Lead SBDC
CALIFORNIA STATE UNIVERSITY - FULLERTON
800 North State College Boulevard, LH640
Fullerton, CA 92834
Phone: 714-278-2719
Fax: 714-278-7858
E-Mail: vpham@fullerton.edu
Website: http://www.leadsbdc.org

California - San Diego SBDC
SOUTHWESTERN COMMUNITY COLLEGE DISTRICT
900 Otay Lakes Road, Bldg. 1681
Chula Vista, CA 91910-7299
Phone: 619-482-6388
Fax: 619-482-6402
E-Mail: dtrujillo@swc.cc.ca.us
Website: http://www.sbditc.org

California - Fresno SBDC
UC Merced Lead Center
UNIVERSITY OF CALIFORNIA - MERCED
550 East Shaw, Suite 100
Fresno, CA 93710-7702
Phone: 559-241-6590
Fax: 559-241-7422
E-Mail: lwright3@ucmerced.edu
Website: http://sbdc.ucmerced.edu

California - Sacramento SBDC
CALIFORNIA STATE UNIVERSITY – CHICO
35 Main Street, Room 203
Chico, CA 95929-0765
Phone: 530-898-4598
Fax: 530-898-4734
E-Mail: dripke@csuchico.edu
Website: http://www.necsbdc.org

California - San Francisco SBDC
Northern California SBDC Lead Center
HUMBOLDT STATE UNIVERSITY
Office of Economic Development
1 Harpst Street
Arcata, CA, 95521
Phone: 707-826-3920
E-Mail: kristin.johnson@humboldt.edu
Website: http://www.norcalsbdc.org

California - Los Angeles Region SBDC
LONG BEACH COMMUNITY COLLEGE DISTRICT
3950 Paramount Boulevard, Ste 101
Lakewood, CA 90712
Phone: 562-938-5004
Fax: 562-938-5030
E-Mail: ssloan@lbcc.edu
Website: www.lasbdcnet.ibcc.edu/lead.html

Colorado SBDC
OFFICE OF ECONOMIC DEVELOPMENT
1625 Broadway, Suite 2700
Denver, CO 80202
Phone: 303-892-3864
Fax: 303-892-3848
E-Mail: Kelly.Manning@state.co.us
Website: http://www.coloradosbdc.org

Connecticut SBDC
University of Central Connecticut
185 Main Street
New Britain, CT 06051
Phone: 860-827-7104
Fax: 860-827-7112
E-Mail: gilmoregin@ccsu.edu
Website: http://www.ccsu.edu/sbdc/

Delaware SBDC
DELAWARE TECHNOLOGY PARK
1 Innovation Way, Suite 301
Newark, DE 19711
Phone: 302-831-1555
Fax: 302-831-1423
E-Mail: tymesc@udel.edu
Website: http://www.delawaresbdc.org

District of Columbia SBDC
HOWARD UNIVERSITY SCHOOL OF BUSINESS
2600 6th Street, NW Room 128
Washington, DC 20059
Phone: 202-806-1550
Fax: 202-806-1777
E-Mail: hturner@howard.edu
Website: http://www.dcsbdc.com/

Florida SBDC
UNIVERSITY OF WEST FLORIDA
401 East Chase Street, Suite 100
Pensacola, FL 32502-6160
Phone: 850-473-7800
Fax: 850-473-7813
E-Mail: jcartwright@uwf.edu
Website: http://www.floridasbdc.com

Georgia SBDC
UNIVERSITY OF GEORGIA
1180 East Broad Street
Athens, GA 30602-5412
Phone: 706-542-2762
Fax: 706-542-7935
E-mail: aadams@georgiasbdc.org
Website: http://www.georgiasbdc.org

Hawaii SBDC
UNIVERSITY OF HAWAII - HILO
308 Kamehameha Avenue, Suite 201
Hilo, HI 96720-2960
Phone: 808-974-7515
Fax: 808-974-7683
E-Mail: darryl.mleynek@hawaii-sbdc.org
Website: http://www.hawaii-sbdc.org

Idaho SBDC
BOISE STATE UNIVERSITY
1910 University Drive
Boise, ID 83725-1655
Phone: 208-426-3799
Fax: 208-426-3877
E-mail: jhogge@boisestate.edu
Website: http://www.idahosbdc.org

Illinois SBDC
DEPARTMENT OF COMMERCE AND ECONOMIC
OPPORTUNITY
620 East Adams Streer, 4th Floor
Springfield, IL 62701-1615
Phone: 217-524-5700
Fax: 217-524-0171
E-mail: mark.petrilli@Illinois.gov
Website: http://www.ilsbdc.biz

Indiana SBDC
INDIANA ECONOMIC DEVELOPMENT CORPORATION
One North Capitol, Suite 900
Indianapolis, IN 46204-2043
Phone: 317-234-2086
Fax: 317-232-8872
E-mail: jheinzmann@ilsbdc.org
Website: http://www.isbdc.org

Iowa SBDC
IOWA STATE UNIVERSITY
340 Gerdin Business Bldg.
Ames, IA 50011-1350
Phone: 515-294-2030
Fax: 515-294-6522
E-mail: jimh@iastate.edu
Website: http://www.iowasbdc.org

Kansas SBDC
FORT HAYS STATE UNIVERSITY
214 SW Sixth Street, Suite 301
Topeka, KS 66603-3719
Phone: 785-296-6514
Fax: 785-291-3261
E-mail: ksbdc.wkearns@fhsu.edu
Website: http://www.fhsu.edu/ksbdc

Kentucky SBDC
UNIVERSITY OF KENTUCKY
225 Gatton College of Business Economics Building
Lexington, KY 40506-0034
Phone: 859-257-7668
Fax: 859-323-1907
E-mail: lrnaug0@uky.edu
Website: http://www.ksbdc.org

Louisiana SBDC
UNIVERSITY OF LOUISIANA - MONROE
College of Business Administration
700 University Avenue
Monroe, LA 71209-6435
Phone: 318-342-5506
Fax: 318-342-5510
E-mail: mlwillkerson@lsbdc.org
Website: http://www.lsbdc.org

Maine SBDC
UNIVERSITY OF SOUTHERN MAINE
96 Falmouth Street P.O. Box 9300
Portland, ME 04103-9300
Phone: 207-780-4420
Fax: 207-780-4810
E-mail: jrmassaua@maine.edu
Website: http://www.mainesbdc.org

Maryland SBDC
UNIVERSITY OF MARYLAND
7100 Baltimore Avenue, Suite 401
College Park, MD 20740-3640
Phone: 301-403-8300 x 15
Fax: 301-403-8303
E-mail: rsprow@mdsbdc.umd.edu
Website: http://www.mdsbdc.umd.edu

Massachusetts SBDC
UNIVERSITY OF MASSACHUSETTS
227 Isenberg School of Management
121 President's Drive
Amherst, MA 01003-9310
Phone: 413-545-6301
Fax: 413-545-1273
E-mail: gep@msbdc.umass.edu
Website: http://www.msbdc.org/

Michigan SBTDC
GRAND VALLEY STATE UNIVERSITY
510 West Fulton Avenue
Grand Rapids, MI 49504
Phone: 616-331-7480
Fax: 616-331-7385
E-mail: sbtdchg@gvsu.edu
Website: http://www.misbtdc.org

Minnesota SBDC
MINNESOTA SMALL BUSINESS DEVELOPMENT CENTER
1st National Bank Building
332 Minnesota Street, Suite E200
St. Paul, MN 55101-1351
Phone: 651-297-5770
Fax: 651-296-5287
E-mail: michael.myhre@state.mn.us
Website: http://www.mnsbdc.com

Mississippi SBDC
UNIVERSITY OF MISSISSIPPI
B-19 Jeanette Phillips Drive
P.O. Box 1848
University, MS 38677-1848
Phone: 662-915-5001
Fax: 662-915-5650
E-mail: wgurley@olemiss.edu
Website: http://www.mssbdc.org

Missouri SBDC
UNIVERSITY OF MISSOURI
410 S. Sixth St.
200 Engineering North
Columbia, MO 65211
Phone: 573-882-0344
Fax: 573-884-4297
E-mail: summersm@missouri.edu
Website: http://www.missouribusiness.net/sbdc/

Montana SBDC
DEPARTMENT OF COMMERCE
301 South Park Avenue, Room 116 / P.O. Box 200505
Helena, MT 59601
Phone: 406-841-27468
Fax: 406-841-2728
E-mail: adesch@mt.gov
Website: http://sbdc.mt.gov/

Nebraska SBDC
UNIVERSITY OF NEBRASKA - OMAHA
415 Roskens Hall
6001 Dodge Street
Omaha, NE 68182 - 0248
Phone: 402-554-2521
Fax: 402-554-3473
E-mail: rbernier@unomaha.edu
Website: http://nbdc.unomaha.edu

Nevada SBDC
UNIVERSITY OF NEVADA - RENO
Reno College of Business
Nazir Ansari Bldg. 032, Rm 4
Reno, NV 89557-0100
Phone: 775-784-1717
Fax: 775-784-4337
E-mail: males@unr.edu
Website: http://www.nsbdc.org

New Hampshire SBDC
UNIVERSITY OF NEW HAMPSHIRE
Mittemore School of Business and Economics, UNH
110 McConnell Hall
Durham, NH 03824-3593
Phone: 603-862-2200
Fax: 603-862-4876
E-mail: Mary.Collins@unh.edu
Website: http://www.nhsbdc.org

New Jersey SBDC
RUTGERS UNIVERSITY
49 Bleeker Street
Newark, NJ 07102-1993
Phone: 973-353-1927
Fax: 973-353-1110
E-mail: bhopper@njsbdc.com
Website: http://www.njsbdc.com/

New Mexico SBDC
SANTA FE COMMUNITY COLLEGE
6401 Richards Avenue
Santa Fe, NM 87508-4887
Phone: 505-428-1362
Fax: 505-428-1469
E-mail: rmiller@sfccnm.edu
Website: http://www.nmsbdc.org

New York SBDC
STATE UNIVERSITY OF NEW YORK
Corporate Woods, 3rd Floor
Albany, NY 12246-0001
Phone: 518-443-5398
Fax: 518-443-5275
E-mail: j.king@nyssbdc.org
Website: http://www.nyssbdc.org

North Carolina SBDTC
UNIVERSITY OF NORTH CAROLINA
5 West Hargett Street, Suite 600
Raleigh, NC 27601-1348
Phone: 919-715-7272
Fax: 919-715-7777
E-mail: sdaugherty@sbtdc.org
Website: http://www.sbtdc.org

North Dakota SBDC
UNIVERSITY OF NORTH DAKOTA
1600 E. Century Avenue, Suite 2
Bismarck, ND 58501
Phone: 701-328-5375
Fax: 701-328-5381
E-mail: bon@ndsbdc.org
Website: http://www.ndsbdc.org

Ohio SBDC
OHIO DEPARTMENT OF DEVELOPMENT
128th Floor
P.O. Box 1001
Columbus, OH 43216-1001
Phone: 614-466-2711
Fax: 614-466-0829
E-mail: mabraham@odod.state.oh.us
Website: entrepreneurohio.org

Oklahoma SBDC
SOUTHEAST OKLAHOMA STATE UNIVERSITY
1405 N 4th Avenue, PMB 2584
Durant, OK 74701-0609
Phone: 580-745-2877 x 2955
Fax: 580-745-7471
E-mail: gpennington@sosu.edu
Website: http://www.osbdc.org

Oregon SBDC
LANE COMMUNITY COLLEGE
99 West Tenth Avenue, Suite 390
Eugene, OR 97401-3015
Phone: 541-463-5250
Fax: 541-345-6006
E-mail: carterb@lanecc.edu
Website: http://www.bizcenter.org

Guam Small Business Development Center
UNIVERSITY OF GUAM
Pacific Islands SBDC
P.O. Box 5014 - U.O.G. Station Mangilao
Mangilao, GU 96923
Phone: 671-735-2590
Fax: 671-734-2002
E-mail: casey@pacificsbdc.com
Website: http://www.pacificsbdc.com

Pennsylvania SBDC
UNIVERSITY OF PENNSYLVANIA
The Wharton School
3733 Spruce Street, Vance Hall, 4th Floor
Philadelphia, PA 19104-6374
Phone: 215-898-1219
Fax: 215-573-2135
E-mail: ghiggins@wharton.upenn.edu
Website: http://pasbdc.org

Puerto Rico SBDC
INTER-AMERICAN UNIVERSITY OF PUERTO RICO
Union Plaza Building, Suite 1000
416 Ponce de Leon Avenue, 10th Floor
Hato Rey, PR 00918
Phone: 787-763-6811
Fax: 787-763-6875
E-mail: cmarti@prsbdc.org
Website: http://www.prsbdc.org

Rhode Island SBDC
JOHNSON & WALES UNIVERSITY
270 Weybosset Street, 4th Floor
Providence, RI 02903
Phone: 401-598-2704
Fax: 401-598-2722
E-mail: john.cronin@jwu.edu
Website: http://www.risbdc.org

South Carolina SBDC
UNIVERSITY OF SOUTH CAROLINA
Darlamoore School of Business
1710 College Street, Hipp Building
Columbia, SC 29208 - 9980
Phone: 803-777-4907
Fax: 803-777-4403
E-mail: lenti@darla.moore.sc.edu
Website: http://scsbdc.moore.sc.edu
South Dakota SBDC
UNIVERSITY OF SOUTH DAKOTA
Beacom School of Business
414 East Clark Street, Patterson Hall
Vermillion, SD 57069
Phone: 605-677-5287Fax: 605-677-5427
E-mail: jshemmin@usd.edu
Website: http://www.sdsbdc.org

Tennessee SBDC
MIDDLE TENNESEE STATE UNIVERSITY
615 Memorial Boulevard
Murfreesboro, TN 37132
Phone: 615-849-9999
Fax: 615-217-8548
E-mail: pgeho@mail.tsbdc.org
Website: http://www.tsbdc.org

Texas-Houston SBDC
UNIVERSITY OF HOUSTON
2302 Fannin, Suite 200
Houston, TX 77002
Phone: 713-752-8444
Fax: 713-756-1500
E-mail: fyoung@uh.edu
Website: http://sbdcnetwork.uh.edu

Texas-North SBDC
DALLAS COUNTY COMMUNITY COLLEGE
1402 Corinth Street, Suite 2111
Dallas, TX 75215
Phone: 214-860-5835
Fax: 214-860-5813
E-mail: emk9402@dcccd.edu
Website: http://www.ntsbdc.org

Texas-NW SBDC
TEXAS TECH UNIVERSITY
2579 South Loop 289, Suite 114
Lubbock, TX 79423-1637
Phone: 806-745-3973
Fax: 806-745-6207
E-mail: c.bean@nwtsbdc.org
Website: http://www.nwtsbdc.org

Texas-South-West Texas Border SBDC Network
UNIVERSITY OF TEXAS – SAN ANTONIO
501 West Durango Boulevard
San Antonio, TX 78207-4415
Phone: 210-458-2450
Fax: 210-458-2425
E-mail: ied@utsa.edu
Website: http://www.txsbdc.org

Utah SBDC
SALT LAKE COMMUNITY COLLEGE
9750 South 300 West - LHM
Salt Lake City, UT 84070
Phone: 801-957-3481
Fax: 801-957-2007E-mail: Greg.Panichello@slcc.edu
Website: http://www.utahsbdc.org/

Vermont SBDC
VERMONT TECHNICAL COLLEGE
PO Box 188, 1 Main Street
Randolph Center, VT 05061-0188
Phone: 802-728-9101
Fax: 802-728-3026
E-mail: lquillen@vtsbdc.org
Website: http://www.vtsbdc.org

Virgin Islands SBDC
UNIVERSITY OF THE VIRGIN ISLANDS
8000 Nisky Center, Suite 720
Charlotte Amalie
St. Thomas, VI 00802-5804
Phone: 340-776-3206
Fax: 340-775-3756
E-mail: ldottin@uvi.edu
Website: http://sbdcvi.org

Virginia SBDC
GEORGE MASON UNIVERSITY
Mason Enterprise Center
4031 University Drive, Suite 200
Fairfax, VA 22030-3409
Phone: 703-277-7727
Fax: 703-352-8518
E-mail: jkeenan@gmu.edu
Website: http://www.virginiasbdc.org

Washington SBDC
WASHINGTON STATE UNIVERSITY
534 E. Spokane Falls Blvd.
P.O. Box 1495
Spokane, WA 99210-1495
Phone: 509-358-7765
Fax: 509-358-7764
E-mail: barogers@wsu.edu
Website: http://www.wsbdc.org

West Virginia SBDC
WEST VIRGINIA DEVELOPMENT OFFICE
1900 Kanawha Blvd. E.
Charleston, WV 25305
Phone: 304-558-2960
Fax: 304-558-0127
E-mail: mgamble@wvsbdc.org
Website: http://www.sbdcwv.org

Wisconsin SBDC
UNIVERSITY OF WISCONSIN
432 North Lake Street, Room 423
Madison, WI 53706
Phone: 608-263-7794
Fax: 608-263-7830
E-mail: debra.malewicki@uwex.edu
Website: http://www.wisconsinsbdc.org

Wyoming SBDC
UNIVERSITY OF WYOMING
1000 E. University, Dept. 3922
Laramie, WY 82979
Phone: 307-766-3505
Fax: 307-766-3406
E-mail: DDW@uwyo.edu
Website: http://www.uwyo.edu/sbdc

# Selected Small Business Forms

# Incident Report Form
*Please complete all information.*

Last Name _____

First Name _____

Social Security No. _____

Date of Birth _____

## Business Information

☐ Employee ☐ Other ☐ Male ☐ Female

Title/Occupation

Phone Extension                    PO Box

## Home Address

_____

Street          City          State          Zip

Phone ( )        _____

Alt. Phone (_____)_____

## Incident Information

Date of incident:_____

Time:_____ ☐ am ☐ pm

Was there a witness? ☐ Yes ☐ No

Name                    Phone ( )                    ext.

Where did the Incident take place? (Please be specific)

_____

What part of the body was injured? (right ankle, left elbow, etc.)


What was the nature of the injury? (Describe the injury, such as bruise, burn, strain, etc.)


What was the source of the injury? (Describe the object, equipment, wet floor, etc. that caused the injury)


Describe what happened (who was involved? When? Where? How? Why?)


Person preparing form (if not the injured party):
Name _____
Title _____
Date prepared _____

# Petty Cash Journal

*Reporting Period*

From _____ To _____

Balance _____

| Date | Voucher # | Account | Account # | Payee | Approved By | Total | Balance |
|------|-----------|---------|-----------|-------|-------------|-------|---------|
|      |           |         |           |       |             |       |         |
|      |           |         |           |       |             |       |         |
|      |           |         |           |       |             |       |         |
|      |           |         |           |       |             |       |         |
|      |           |         |           |       |             |       |         |
|      |           |         |           |       |             |       |         |
|      |           |         |           |       |             |       |         |
|      |           |         |           |       |             |       |         |
|      |           |         |           |       |             |       |         |
|      |           |         |           |       |             |       |         |
|      |           |         |           |       |             |       |         |
|      |           |         |           |       |             |       |         |
|      |           |         |           |       |             |       |         |
|      |           |         |           |       |             |       |         |
|      |           |         |           |       |             |       |         |
|      |           |         |           |       |             |       |         |

Audited By _____

Approved By _____

| | Total | Balance |
|---|---|---|
| Total Voucher Amount | | |
| Total Receipts | | |
| Cash on Hand | | |
| Overage/Shortage | | |
| Petty Cash Reimbursement | | |
| Balance Forward | | |

# Aging of Accounts Payable

## Reporting Period

From _____ To _____

| | | | | | Amount | | | |
|---|---|---|---|---|---|---|---|---|
| Date | Invoice # | Account | Account # | Description | *30 Days* | 60 Days | 90+ Days | Total |
| | | | | | | | | |
| | | | | | | | | |
| | | | | | | | | |
| | | | | | | | | |
| | | | | | | | | |
| | | | | | | | | |
| | | | | | | | | |
| | | | | | | | | |
| | | | | | | | | |
| | | | | | | | | |
| | | | | | | | | |
| | | | | | | | | |
| | | | | | | | | |
| | | | | | | | | |
| | | | | | | | | |
| | | | | | | | | |
| | | | | | | | | |
| | | | | | | | | |
| | | | | | | | | |
| | | | | | | | | |
| | | | | | | | | |

# Aging of Accounts Receivable

## Reporting Period:

From _____ To _____

| | | | | | Amount | | | |
|---|---|---|---|---|---|---|---|---|
| Date | Invoice # | Account | Account # | Description | 30 Days | 60 Days | 90+ Days | Total |
| | | | | | | | | |
| | | | | | | | | |
| | | | | | | | | |
| | | | | | | | | |
| | | | | | | | | |
| | | | | | | | | |
| | | | | | | | | |
| | | | | | | | | |
| | | | | | | | | |
| | | | | | | | | |
| | | | | | | | | |
| | | | | | | | | |
| | | | | | | | | |
| | | | | | | | | |
| | | | | | | | | |
| | | | | | | | | |
| | | | | | | | | |
| | | | | | | | | |
| | | | | | | | | |
| | | | | | | | | |
| | | | | | | | | |

# Auto Expense Travel Report

Date: _____

| Employee Name | Completed By |
|---|---|
| Location Dept. | Audited By |
| Address | Purpose of Trip |
| City State ZIP | Approved By |
| Phone | Approved By |

| Date | Travel From | Travel To | Odometer | | Total Mileage | Rate/ Mile | Amount Due |
|---|---|---|---|---|---|---|---|
| | | | Start | End | | | |
| | | | | | | | |
| | | | | | | | |
| | | | | | | | |
| | | | | | | | |
| | | | | | | | |
| | | | | | | | |
| | | | | | | | |
| | | | | | | | |
| | | | | | | *Total* | |
| Less Cash Advance | | | | | | | |
| Less Charges to Company | | | | | | | |
| Total Balance Due | | | | | | | |

# Cash Disbursements Journal

Month _____

General Ledger Number _____

| Date | Check # | Payee | Account Credited | Account # | Cash | Discount | Other | Account Debited | Account # | Amount Payable | Other |
|------|---------|-------|------------------|-----------|------|----------|-------|-----------------|-----------|----------------|-------|
|      |         |       |                  |           |      |          |       |                 |           |                |       |
|      |         |       |                  |           |      |          |       |                 |           |                |       |
|      |         |       |                  |           |      |          |       |                 |           |                |       |
|      |         |       |                  |           |      |          |       |                 |           |                |       |
|      |         |       |                  |           |      |          |       |                 |           |                |       |
|      |         |       |                  |           |      |          |       |                 |           |                |       |
|      |         |       |                  |           |      |          |       |                 |           |                |       |
|      |         |       |                  |           |      |          |       |                 |           |                |       |
|      |         |       |                  |           |      |          |       |                 |           |                |       |
|      |         |       |                  |           |      |          |       |                 |           |                |       |
|      |         |       |                  |           |      |          |       |                 |           |                |       |
|      |         |       |                  |           |      |          |       |                 |           |                |       |
|      |         |       |                  |           |      |          |       |                 |           |                |       |
|      |         |       |                  |           |      |          |       |                 |           |                |       |
|      |         |       |                  |           |      |          |       |                 |           |                |       |
|      |         |       |                  |           |      |          |       |                 |           |                |       |
|      |         |       |                  |           |      |          |       |                 |           |                |       |

# Cash Receipts Journal

Month _____

General Ledger Number _____

| Date | Account Credited | Account # | Sales | Amount Receivable | Other | Account Debited | Account # | Cash | Discounts | Other |
|------|------------------|-----------|-------|-------------------|-------|-----------------|-----------|------|-----------|-------|
|      |                  |           |       |                   |       |                 |           |      |           |       |
|      |                  |           |       |                   |       |                 |           |      |           |       |
|      |                  |           |       |                   |       |                 |           |      |           |       |
|      |                  |           |       |                   |       |                 |           |      |           |       |
|      |                  |           |       |                   |       |                 |           |      |           |       |
|      |                  |           |       |                   |       |                 |           |      |           |       |
|      |                  |           |       |                   |       |                 |           |      |           |       |
|      |                  |           |       |                   |       |                 |           |      |           |       |
|      |                  |           |       |                   |       |                 |           |      |           |       |
|      |                  |           |       |                   |       |                 |           |      |           |       |
|      |                  |           |       |                   |       |                 |           |      |           |       |
|      |                  |           |       |                   |       |                 |           |      |           |       |
|      |                  |           |       |                   |       |                 |           |      |           |       |
|      |                  |           |       |                   |       |                 |           |      |           |       |
|      |                  |           |       |                   |       |                 |           |      |           |       |
|      |                  |           |       |                   |       |                 |           |      |           |       |

# Daily Cash Report

Date _____
Page _____
Of _____

| # | Cash Recorded From | Amount | Cash Paid Out To | Amount |
|---|---|---|---|---|
|   |   |   |   |   |
|   |   |   |   |   |
|   |   |   |   |   |
|   |   |   |   |   |
|   |   |   |   |   |
|   |   |   |   |   |
|   |   |   |   |   |
|   |   |   |   |   |
|   |   |   |   |   |
|   |   |   |   |   |
|   |   |   |   |   |
|   |   |   |   |   |
|   |   |   |   |   |
|   |   |   |   |   |
|   |   |   |   |   |
| Total Cash Received |   |   | Total Cash Paid Out |   |
| Notes |   |   |   |   |
|   |   |   | Total Receipts | $ |
|   |   |   | Less Cash Out | $ |
|   |   |   | Balance | $ |

# General Journal

Month _____

General Ledger Number_____

| Date | Amount Debited | Account Number | Amount | Account Credited | Account Number | Amount |
|------|----------------|----------------|--------|------------------|----------------|--------|
|      |                |                |        |                  |                |        |
|      |                |                |        |                  |                |        |
|      |                |                |        |                  |                |        |
|      |                |                |        |                  |                |        |
|      |                |                |        |                  |                |        |
|      |                |                |        |                  |                |        |
|      |                |                |        |                  |                |        |
|      |                |                |        |                  |                |        |
|      |                |                |        |                  |                |        |
|      |                |                |        |                  |                |        |
|      |                |                |        |                  |                |        |
|      |                |                |        |                  |                |        |
|      |                |                |        |                  |                |        |
|      |                |                |        |                  |                |        |
|      |                |                |        |                  |                |        |
|      |                |                |        |                  |                |        |
|      |                |                |        |                  |                |        |
|      |                |                |        |                  |                |        |
|      |                |                |        |                  |                |        |
|      |                |                |        |                  |                |        |
|      |                |                |        |                  |                |        |
|      |                |                |        |                  |                |        |
|      |                |                |        |                  |                |        |

## Petty Cash Vouchers

| Account | Description | Amount |
|---|---|---|
|  |  |  |
|  |  |  |
|  |  |  |
|  |  |  |
|  |  |  |
|  |  |  |
|  |  |  |
|  |  |  |
|  |  |  |
|  |  |  |
|  |  |  |
|  |  |  |
|  |  |  |
|  |  |  |
|  |  |  |
|  |  |  |
|  |  |  |
|  |  |  |
|  |  |  |
|  |  |  |
|  | Total Cash Amount | $ |

Voucher # _____

Received by _____

Authorized by_____

# Financial Ratios

| Ratio | Formula |
|---|---|
| Acid test (quick) | (Current assets – Inventory)/Current liabilities |
| Collection period | Accounts receivable/Working capital |
| Current liabilities to owner's equity | Current liabilities/Owners' equity |
| Current ratio | Current assets/Current liabilities |
| Debt to owners' equity | Total liabilities/Owner's equity |
| Fixed assets to owners' equity | Fixed assets/Owners' equity |
| Inventory to working capital | Inventory/Working capital |
| Long-term liabilities to working capital | Long-term liabilities/Working capital |
| Net sales to fixed assets | Net sales/Fixed assets |
| Net profit owners' equity | Net profit before taxes/Owners' equity |
| Net profit to net sales | Net profit before taxes/Net sales |
| Net sales to owners' equity | Net sales/ Owners' equity |
| Net sales to working capital | Net sales/ Working capital |
| Net sales to inventory | Net sales/Inventory |
| Receivables to working capital | Accounts receivables/Working capital |

Purchase Order

Submitted by: _____

Order Number_____

Date ordered: _____

Date Required: _____

Ship to: Joseph Brown
    ABC Corporation.
    10003 North Avenue
    Brooklyn, NY 11235
    Tel. (718) 999-9999

Please supply and deliver the goods or services
specified below to the address above.

| Item No. | Quantity | Description | Net Unit Price | *Total* |
|---|---|---|---|---|
|  |  |  |  |  |
|  |  |  |  |  |
|  |  |  |  |  |
|  |  |  |  |  |
|  |  |  |  |  |
|  |  |  |  |  |
|  |  |  |  |  |
|  |  |  |  |  |
|  |  |  |  |  |
| *Net Total Price* |  |  |  | $ |

Invoices, quoting the order number, should be submitted for payment to:

Name _____

Title _____

This order is not valid unless it is signed. Please acknowledge receipt of this order.

Approved:_____

Date:_____

# PROMISSORY NOTE

Date: _____

This is to acknowledge that

_____

has borrowed _____dollars

$_____

From

Last Name_____

First Name_____

Address: _____
        *Number    Street   Apt. /Suite     City   State   Zip*

Tel: _____ Cell: _____
Email_____

For value received, the Borrower promises to pay to the Noteholder,

_____,

a) ___ Consecutive installment of $_____ per
___day, _____week, _____every two weeks, ____month, ____year,
___other (specify) _____,
until paid in full.

b) ___In full on or before_____.

    This note may be prepaid in whole or in part at any time without penalty. In the event of any default, the Borrower will be responsible for any costs of collection on this note, including court costs and attorney fees. However, the Noteholder may facilitate payment arrangement with the borrower.

_____ _____

Signature of Borrower / Date Name of Borrower
 Acting on behalf of: _____